FENG

SHUI

AT

WORK

VILLARD · NEW YORK

FENG SHUI AT WORK

ARRANGING YOUR WORK SPACE FOR PEAK PERFORMANCE AND MAXIMUM PROFIT

KIRSTEN M. LAGATREE

Illustrations by Lillian Langotsky

Library of Congress Cataloging-in-Publication Data

Lagatree, Kirsten M.
Feng shui at work : arranging your work space for peak
performance and maximum profit / Kirsten M. Lagatree.
p.   cm.
ISBN 0-375-75010-X (alk. paper)
1. Feng shui.   2. Quality of work life.   I. Title.
BF1779.F4L343   1998
133.3'337—dc21   97-44828

Random House website address: www.randomhouse.com
Printed in the United States of America on acid-free paper
98765432
First Edition
Book design by JoAnne Metsch

This book is dedicated with love to
Marion, Donald, and Bruce Lagatree

ACKNOWLEDGMENTS

I'D LIKE to say thank you to Monte Durham, Kitty Felde, John-dennis Govert, and Jami Lin, whose generous assistance meant a great deal to me on this project. And special thanks to Professor Louis G. Perez of Illinois State University for his guidance on questions of Chinese history, culture, and language. Appreciation also goes to my editor, Page Edmunds, and to Kirsten Raymond at Villard. Suzanne Wickham-Beaird, the West Coast editor of Villard, deserves special mention, because her vision launched this project more than three years ago, and her enthusiasm and energy have propelled it ever since. Affectionate thanks to my pal Rick Koonce for being a good listener and for reminding me of the importance of going out to lunch once in a while. Finally, love and thanks to my husband, John Barth, who is responsible for the good feng shui at our house.

CONTENTS

INTRODUCTION

HOW DO you feel when you walk into your office each morning? Are you energized and ready to work, brimming with creative ideas for the day ahead? Or do you feel tired even before you start the day, or a bit demoralized as you anticipate the tasks in front of you? It may surprise you to know that these feelings can have more to do with your work space than with your job description, your boss, or your co-workers.

Your surroundings have a powerful effect on how you feel and behave, whether you're at home, at the doctor's office, at a party, or at work. But because work is such an important part of life—taking up about half your waking hours—your office environment is especially critical.

Even when you're not at work, the quality of your life is often dictated by the quality of the work you do. Your finances, your self-esteem, your value in the eyes of others: All are frequently determined by the type and quality of your labors.

Your office space and its arrangement are as important to the work you do as a wrench is to a plumber, a scalpel to a surgeon, or a notebook to a writer. Whether your work space is a large corporate office, a tiny cubicle, or a corner of your dining room table, it must be in harmony and balance with nature to be conducive to your productivity.

By controlling your work environment through feng shui, the ancient Chinese art of placement, you are taking charge of your professional destiny. When you arrange your office according to the rules of feng shui, you can boost your finances, improve your reputation, build your business, enhance your creativity, and even improve your relationships with co-workers.

In this book you will meet several professional people whose jobs or careers have been positively affected by the practice of feng shui. As I listened to their experiences, I gained a new appreciation of the extent to which feng shui can change our lives. This ancient art brings results.

My own extraordinary experience with feng shui began in the early months of 1992. As a freelance writer and regular contributor to the *Los Angeles Times*, I called my editor one day, eager to suggest a special story I wanted to write. I'd planned to tell him about a fascinating subject I'd recently heard about: feng shui. But he stopped me before I could get to my pitch and said, "Whatever story you have in mind will have to wait. There's another one I want you to work on right away." Then he told me he wanted a story about feng shui. I was stunned, and for a few seconds couldn't reply. When I gathered my wits, I told him that was the exact idea I had for him.

What began as a slightly eerie coincidence turned out to be the highly auspicious beginning of a series of events that would change my life.

As I was researching and writing that *Los Angeles Times* article about the ways feng shui was changing the Southern California real estate market, my husband and I were moving into a new home. Moving is always hectic and somewhat chaotic, and I found it difficult to continue my writing while we camped out with cardboard boxes in the new house. But even after I was settled into my large new home office, I found it hard to concentrate on my writing and even harder to come up with fresh, clear ideas for what I knew should be a great story. In addition, I just didn't feel comfortable at my desk. But I couldn't put my finger on what the problem might be.

Feeling frustrated, I asked my husband to help me rearrange my new office. I had placed my desk so that it faced a window, thinking that my view of the backyard would allow me to concentrate on my work. But when my husband stepped in, he moved the desk to the other side of the room, positioning it so I could see the door while I wrote. His innate sense of good design told him that this was a better arrangement. For reasons I didn't yet understand, I began to feel more powerful while seated at my desk and more in control of my writing assignment. Suddenly, it felt *great* to be working in that room!

As I did more research about feng shui, I began to see that John's rearrangement of my office had improved the feng shui of the room. As it turned out, the good feng shui of my office not only enhanced my ability to work but exerted a powerful influence over the direction of my professional life.

When the *Los Angeles Times* article appeared, it generated a good deal of interest from readers. Among them was the West Coast editor for Villard Books, who called with an offer most freelance writers only dream about: Might I be interested in delving deeper into the subject and writing a good, basic handbook about feng shui? This was the opportunity of a lifetime: to write a book on a subject I knew had the potential to affect the lives of thousands of readers in a positive fashion, just as it had begun to affect mine. I knew I owed some of my success to feng shui itself.

Is there a lesson here for you? Yes. When he rearranged my office, my husband had no knowledge of feng shui, but his instincts led to good feng shui. In striving for a work atmosphere of comfort and convenience, he had unconsciously made the kind of changes that the practice of feng shui suggests, improving the room's balance, harmony, and energy flow. This experience made clear to me a basic tenet of feng shui: A room with good design—one that is comfortable and functional—is usually one with good feng shui. As you use this book to rearrange your work space, trust your own intuition. Like John, you may know more than you think you do about feng shui.

FENG
SHUI
AT
WORK

1

WHAT IS FENG SHUI?

FENG SHUI is the ancient Chinese art of placement. Think of it as acupuncture for a building. Just as the acupuncturist adjusts the body's energy flow with needles, the feng shui practitioner uses objects to redirect the flow of energy through an indoor or outdoor environment. The acupuncturist's skills yield a healthy patient; the feng shui master's efforts create a balanced and healthy environment. Both add immeasurably to the quality of human life.

Put most simply, feng shui is a system for arranging your surroundings so they are in harmony and balance with nature. When your surroundings are serene and in harmony with powerful universal forces, so are you. And so is your life.

The principles of feng shui can be applied to the placement of a vase of flowers or to the drawing of an entire architectural plan. With proper feng shui you can tilt the balance in your life toward financial success, improved relationships, enhanced creativity—whatever goals you may have. As you learn about feng shui and begin to practice its techniques, you'll have more control over your life and you'll gain an edge in your personal and professional endeavors.

WIND AND
WATER

IN CHINESE, the words "feng shui" mean "wind and water." These two elements stand as a metaphor for the power of nature in our world and the absolute importance of respecting that power as we arrange the details of our daily lives. Good feng shui design uses natural elements and echoes the patterns of nature—the curve of landscapes, the flow of wind, the movement of water—as it balances the universal forces that affect our destiny.

WHERE IT
COMES FROM

ABOUT THREE thousand years ago, farmers in southern China began to take note of certain facts in their daily lives.

They observed that crops planted on the windward side of a hill became parched and dry or were destroyed altogether by seemingly merciless natural forces. Battered by winds and unprotected from driving rains, fragile rice and bean plants shriveled. Those that managed to grow were far from robust. In these "windward years" when harvests were skimpy, feeding the family—let alone growing enough food to barter for other goods—was a difficult proposition.

The poverty, hunger, sickness, and death that ensued gradually took their toll on everyone, whether they were farmers or not. As it became clear that prosperity and even life expectancy were directly related to the choice of where and how to plant, the importance of living in harmony with nature loomed very large indeed.

These rural dwellers also observed that families whose huts faced north took the brunt of ferocious dust storms blowing down from the Gobi Desert. Every time they walked out their north-facing doors, grit lashed their faces, sand stung their eyes, and dirt swept into their homes, settling onto bedding and cooking utensils. South-facing huts, on the other hand, were a source of good fortune for their occupants; not only were these inhabitants protected from the harsh effects of dust storms, they enjoyed the added benefit of warmth and light from the sun that came streaming in the front door.

The farmers' discovery that facing south brought them good fortune, a more pleasant life, and many other blessings gradually gave that compass point special status. In fact, because feng shui was always carefully observed in siting and building imperial palaces, the Chinese have a saying, "To face south is to become a king." To this day, south is considered to be a most auspicious direction, governing fame, fortune, and festivity—some of life's most sought-after blessings.

These and dozens of other simple observations gradually evolved into a set of principles governing every aspect of life *and* life after death. Ancestor veneration is an important part of Chinese culture, and feng shui was—and in many cases still is—extremely important for finding the best burial sites for family members. In ancient China, feng shui experts, or geomancers, were called upon to help bury the dead. Forebears who are properly and carefully buried are thought to look more kindly on their living relatives, watching over them and bestowing the blessings of prosperity, honor, long life, and healthy offspring.

SCHOOLS OF FENG SHUI

IN ITS development over the past two millennia, the art and science of feng shui has been adapted to suit different environments and cultures. There are three major schools now, and their methods are being practiced throughout the world, none in a strictly pure form. Each school uses at least a little something from the others.

The Land Form School followed the observations of the ancient farmers and was the first kind of feng shui practiced. In those early days of feng shui, wise men in southern China used hills, mountains, rivers, lakes, and other geographical points to guide them in siting villages, palaces, and burial grounds. They tried to find sites where surrounding hills and mountains would provide shelter from wind and weather, and they looked for hills that resembled the shapes of dragons, tigers, and tortoises—creatures they believed would provide the inhabitants of the area with celestial gifts and protection.

The dragon was the most revered of these creatures because it represented the greatest power and therefore the best protection. Its moods could bring about terrible destruction or great blessings. Droughts resulted from unhappy, thirsty dragons, and catastrophes such as floods and typhoons were caused by angry, malevolent dragons. On the other hand, a happy, satisfied dragon sent gentle showers to nourish crops, and its benevolence kept disasters at bay.

Sites near "dragon hills" were sought after as sacred and advantageous locations. An ideal spot would have hills that resembled a green dragon on the east, a slope resembling the fiercely protective white tiger to the west, and a range of smaller hillocks symbolizing the black tortoise to the north. In this position a building (or village) is nestled in a geologic armchair, with back and sides suggesting comfort as well as protection.

These special locations were determined by highly subjective decisions made by the feng shui master and respectfully followed by everyone from humble villagers to mighty emperors. The Land Form School is very intuitive, relying mainly on the interpretation of metaphors and symbols. While other schools added more concrete rules, today's feng shui still requires a significant amount of intuition. That is why a truly great feng shui master must have special talent as well as years of study.

Ideal Building Placement Between Dragon and Tiger Hills

Gradually the practice of feng shui spread beyond southern China (with its dramatic and easily distinguished land forms) and into the flat plains of central and northern China. Lacking physical clues in the landscape, geomancers began to take a more formulaic approach in determining auspicious locations. Instead of relying completely on the landscape, they began to use compass directions, combined with metaphysics, astrology, complex mathematical calculations, and an eight-sided chart, known as the ba-gua, to do their work. What developed became known as the Compass School.

About fifty years ago, Chinese American feng shui master Thomas Lin Yun established a third major school to provide a more accessible, less complicated approach for Westerners. The Black Hat Sect Tantric Tibetan Buddhist School, or BTB, doesn't use compass directions at all. Instead, it uses the front door of a building or room as the orientation point for determining relevant and favorable directions. Today both the Compass and BTB schools have many followers.

This book is based on an updated and clarified compass method, distilled with the help of feng shui expert Angi Ma Wong. Like the BTB approach, this system has been refined for a Western audience, and like the Land Form School, it calls upon the intuition of the practitioner to help determine what works best for each situation. It has the precision and clarity of the Compass School, the integration of natural forces of the Land Form School, and the practicality and accessibility required by Western users.

This method will allow you to choose from a variety of options in designing and arranging your environment. You will be able to select the feng shui adjustments that fit your own requirements and tastes. In fact, it's essential to pay attention to your reactions and feelings as you work your way through the book, always choosing an option that feels right to you.

CHI

THERE ARE some elements all feng shui schools have in common, and the most important one is chi. The Chinese sometimes refer to chi as the cosmic dragon's breath of the universe, but chi can be understood more readily as energy or the life force. Chi is in the air, constantly circulating around us and influencing everything from our health to our prosperity to our propensity for misfortune and illness. Like electricity, chi is an invisible but powerful force in our everyday lives.

The goal of good feng shui is to harness this vital force to maximize the positive effects it bestows. By enhancing and directing chi flow, we are able to direct our fate in a positive way.

A natural force, chi moves most beneficially around curves, preferring the gentle shapes that occur in nature to the sharp angles of man-made designs. When it flows in a curving path, chi travels at a leisurely pace, bestowing its powerful life force and blessings as it goes. Straight lines or sharp angles cause it to move too quickly, resulting in "poison arrows" that have harmful effects. Man-made structures that reshape the environment—roads, tunnels, housing developments, and so forth—can adversely affect its movement, creating bad chi, called sha.

Imagine good chi as the wind, blowing gently through trees, creating cooling, refreshing breezes and clean, healthful air. But picture the wind rushing through an urban canyon, along a block of skyscrapers, knocking the breath from you as you step off the curb, and you'll see the difference between positive and negative chi flow.

Unfortunately, negative chi is fairly common in offices and other workplaces. Long narrow corridors can create sha chi, bringing any number of business, health, or relationship problems. The sharp angles created by filing cabinets, cubicles, and square columns set poison arrows flying around a workplace, unleashing vicious office politics, bringing on head- or backaches and a host of other physical or psychological maladies to office inhabitants.

While sha chi and poison arrows can result from sharp angles or long narrow passages where chi flows too quickly, physical obstructions blocking its path can also cause problems resulting from stagnant chi. When furniture impedes free activity in a room or when a tree blocks easy access to a building, chi flow is interrupted. Chi can also become blocked by everyday clutter: stacks of paper, boxes, files—whatever you've got piled up. Stagnant chi cuts you off from all the positive benefits of free-flowing energy and can bring about problems in areas ranging from health to relationships. Stagnant chi, particularly in a work environment, can interfere with creativity, focus, and concentration.

If you have an area where stagnant chi seems to be a chronic problem, add something from this list of items that readily attract chi.

Light
Water (particularly moving water, as in fish tanks and fountains)
Living things (fish, pets, birds)
Plants and flowers
Reflections (mirrors)
Movement (ceiling fans, wind chimes)
Bold colors
Crystals
Beautiful art objects

Any object that catches your eye in a pleasant way will attract positive chi.

But just as too much of any good thing can plague us in life, too much chi can cause problems. If, for instance, you're having trouble focusing or concentrating, check your work area for signs of too much chi. For example, clear light is helpful in maintaining a room's good chi. But overbright or harsh light (a common situation in many workplaces) can make the chi too intense and will be overpowering and stressful.

PERSONAL CHI

JUST AS the chi in our environment affects our fate, our personal chi animates us and makes us who we are. When you meet a highly charismatic person, you are looking at someone with powerful personal chi. A person with vibrant, healthy chi is enthusiastic, energetic, and ready to take on new projects; such a person attracts people with that special air of energy and confidence. People lacking good chi, on the other hand, may feel lethargic, depressed, or unable to face the future with confidence. They tend to put people off rather than attract them. You do have a degree of control over your personal chi. Taking care of yourself with proper food, sleep, and exercise will give you a head start on feeling energetic, enthusiastic, and confident. A healthy lifestyle leads to healthy chi.

Manipulating your environment to create good external chi flow and good feng shui will help you achieve your goals. But in order to set those goals in the first place, you'll benefit from the vitality and optimism that come with good individual chi. As you begin to comprehend the flow and interplay of personal and environmental chi, your practice of feng shui will become more successful.

YIN AND YANG

BECAUSE FENG shui stems from science as well as art, it is a bit more easily understood from the perspective of the Chinese view of the cosmos. At the center of this philosophy is the concept of yin and yang. These opposite forces shape this universe and everything in it; together they make up a balanced whole. Yin is female, yang is male. Yin is represented by the stealthy tiger. Yang is like the dragon— fierce, strong, hot, moving, and active. Don't think of these opposite forces as "good" and "bad." They are actually complementary. Both are necessary to the universe, and they depend on each other for their very existence. Without night there is no day. Without death there is no life.

Together yin and yang comprise the Tao (pronounced "dow"), which means "the way" or "the path." The interaction of these two

Everything in the universe contains some yin and some yang. Note the dot of white (yang) within the black yin symbol and vice versa. When yin and yang are pictured inside a circle, this is the Taichi symbol of completeness.

forces creates chi and makes the world work the way it does (summer turns into winter, night becomes day). Balancing these forces is at the heart of the practice of feng shui. When we achieve that balance we find that our life is in harmony and our fortunes take a turn for the better.

Yin/Yang Qualities

Yin is the tiger	Yang is the dragon
Yin is the earth	Yang is the heaven
Yin is the moon	Yang is the sun
Yin is the winter	Yang is the summer
Yin is the mother	Yang is the father
Yin is the lake	Yang is the mountain
Yin is cold	Yang is heat
Yin is rain	Yang is sunshine
Yin is odd numbers	Yang is even numbers
Yin is meekness	Yang is aggression
Yin is plants	Yang is rocks
Yin is rounded	Yang is sharp-angled
Yin is quiet	Yang is noisy

The more you understand these complementary forces—and the ways they manifest themselves in every part of your world—the better you will be at achieving good feng shui. This is especially important for your workplace, since there are naturally many yang forces at play there (aggression, hard surfaces, bright lights), and you must be alert to the need for yin elements to create that perfect universal (and less stressful) balance.

David Starkweather is a smart and resourceful development director for a large nonprofit enterprise. But he was having trouble getting started as soon as he arrived at work in the morning. He was full of energy and had lots of good ideas, but he felt scattered and unable to focus on one thing at a time or even stick to the to-do list he'd made the night before.

He consulted a feng shui practitioner who immediately linked an excess of chi in David's east-facing office with his overstimulated brain. Not only were fluorescent lights bearing down brightly on him, the morning and early afternoon sun came pouring through his window. He was lucky enough to have a coveted view of the mountains from this window, but those hard masculine land forms brought too much yang into his office.

The feng shui practitioner put a translucent shade on the window to block some of the excess light and obscure the view of the mountains. He also placed a banker's lamp on David's desk. Although the lamp added light to an already bright room, the soft glow dispersed the chi gently throughout the room. The pool of light also helped David focus on the work in front of him. The green lampshade brought a sense of calm and coolness to the room, and the lamp made David's office seem just a bit more personal. It made an enormous difference in his mood while he worked.

Yin/Yang theory is different from our conventional Western way of looking at the world, which tends toward labeling things "good" or "bad" and looking for black-and-white answers. Yin/Yang theory is highly attuned to the constantly changing nature of the universe. It makes room for opposites and always seeks to balance them. It is non-judgmental and leads to a live-and-let-live worldview. Absorbing this concept will give you an advantage in business: You'll always have the broader perspective and take a longer view.

2

SETTING YOUR GOALS

MOST OF us have to work for a living. Some of us enjoy it at least part of the time. But even when you like your job, there are obstacles to getting the most from it: lack of concentration, difficult colleagues, blocked creativity. If you often feel that work is an uphill battle, a chore, or a necessary evil, you may be pleasantly surprised at the changes feng shui can bring about in your workplace and, as a result, in your level of job satisfaction.

Take a moment right now and picture yourself thriving on your work—imagine feeling powerful, creative, productive, and appreciated more of the time. Think how much better Monday mornings would feel!

DETERMINING YOUR GOALS

THE BEST, most effective way to change your life with feng shui is to know exactly what you want to accomplish. Only then can you use the art and science of feng shui to maximum advantage. This chapter will walk you through the basics of determining your goals.

Before you begin working with chi and the ba-gua, you must have a clear idea of what you'd like to accomplish. You can have the practice of feng shui nailed down to a science, but if you don't choose a goal—whether getting a raise or starting a new business—and set out deliberately to achieve it, you won't get very far. As veteran interior designer and feng shui practitioner Jami Lin puts it, "Intention is everything!"

What do you want most from your job? Do you wish you made more money? Do you crave creativity? Or do you long for greater autonomy? Perhaps you'd like to take a stronger leadership role. Or maybe you're feeling discontented with your job or your role in the workplace, but you aren't sure just what kind of change would constitute improvement. The possibilities for change are so numerous and varied that it can be difficult to pinpoint exactly where to start.

Gathering critical information about your current work situation and your goals will enable you to select the feng shui adjustments and enhancements that fit smoothly with your needs. The most powerful feng shui adjustments are quite specific to a carefully chosen goal. And the most successful feng shui enhancements are highly personal, tailored as closely as possible to your personality, your professional aspirations, and even your personal taste. The exercises that follow will help you isolate problems, uncover your aspirations, focus on goals and objectives, and set priorities, so you can make feng shui work better for you.

TAKING STOCK

TAKE A piece of paper and divide it into two columns. In the left column, jot down the things you like about your life. Include large and small things; don't confine your list to your career, and don't be afraid to count both large and small joys, such as good friendships, a green thumb, a dog you love, or a talent for Trivial Pursuit.

In the right column, make a list of all those areas of your professional life you'd like to improve. If you're dissatisfied with your job, be specific (don't like the boss, find the work dull, don't see chance for advancement, etc.). Work quickly at first, so that your answers come as much as possible from your subconscious. Don't judge yourself as you write. Put the list away and come back to it the following day, adding new items that have occurred to you. Keep this list with you — use it as a bookmark. It will ground, enlighten, and direct you as you decide exactly what you want to change about your professional life.

GO QUICKLY through the checklists below, again trying to elicit your most honest response. When you finish a list, check your score at the end. Write down what you learn from the score results of each list. Compare these observations with the two-column list you created in the earlier exercise.

QUALITY·OF·LIFE EXERCISES

You will begin to see a pattern emerging that will help you focus on important issues and develop priorities for the changes you wish to make.

Physical Surroundings

The point of this exercise is to find out what ordinary changes you may have to make before you begin to improve the feng shui of your work area.

Answer yes or no:
1. When I arrive at work, I like what I see
2. My desk/work station makes it easy to be productive
3. I feel physically comfortable while working
4. My work area contains personal objects that are important to me
5. I'm organized and in control of the papers and other items I need to do my job

If you answered no to even one of the statements, your first priority is to make a few strictly practical changes in your physical surroundings. Be on the lookout for cramped conditions, poor lighting, or physical obstructions. Also, be sure to read the section on clutter in chapter 4.

Psychological Environment

No one feels the same way every day, so choose the answer that seems to be true most often. Do the best you can to respond to these statements quickly and honestly.

Respond yes or no:

1. When people come to my office/work area, they often say it feels good to be there
2. While working, I'm able to focus clearly and concentrate well
3. I feel competent in performing my job
4. I feel confident as I approach new tasks
5. My interactions with co-workers are generally positive
6. I get along with my boss
7. The work day usually goes by quickly for me
8. My work generally receives the recognition it deserves
9. My work assignments are interesting and challenging
10. I am given the freedom to do my job as I see fit

If you responded no to more than three of the above statements, you have serious feng shui problems in your current office. You need to isolate and correct the negative energy around you. Some of your changes will be transcendental cures—more subtle and intuitive, but no less important than the practical changes you made to organize your physical surroundings.

PATH OF
CHI EXERCISE

AFTER YOU'VE looked inward at your areas of contentment or unhappiness and have begun to formulate an idea of what you want to accomplish, take a careful look at your surroundings. Go outside the building where you work. Start at the path to the front door, walk slowly up to and through the entrance, and make your way through the building and out the exit. As you go, be attuned to your intuitive sense of the energy flow. This will do two things: It will outline the path of chi through the building and show you where the heaviest traffic areas are.

Start by clearing away any obstacles you find in the path of chi. Is there a piece of furniture blocking chi flow near the entrance? Do you have file cabinets or large bookcases that prevent chi from flowing through important areas? Maybe your own office has file boxes stacked in the way, inhibiting your own free movement (and therefore your achievements) every single day?

It could be that you haven't noticed these things before because you're so used to seeing them and walking around them. But even though you aren't conscious of them on a daily basis, they are definitely taking their toll on your career success and personal well-being.

Empty those boxes, move that filing cabinet, clear out those stacks of paper overwhelming or blocking your creativity. Once you've cleared the way—both physically and psychologically—you're ready to begin planning for the future. You will find details on how to do this in the clutter section of chapter 4.

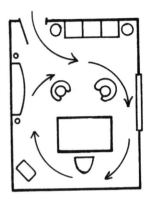

The arrangement of your office should allow chi to flow freely.

THE FUTURE

THE CHANGES and adjustments you make to improve your current situation will also have an impact on your future. This section will direct your thinking a little farther down the road. Circle one or more:

In five years, I would like to be:
1. working at a different job I currently have in mind
2. in a more responsible job in my current line of work
3. working out of an office at home
4. staying home with my children
5. I have no idea where I'd like to be in five years
6. other _____

If you circled 1, 2, 3, 4, or 6, because you already have a clear idea of what you'd like to be doing in five years, write it down and post your goal where you can see it every day.

If you chose 5, you might want to consider talking with a career counselor. Richard Koonce, author of *Career Power: 12 Winning Habits to Get You from Where You Are to Where You Want to Be*, recommends a counselor as a very important sounding board for anyone looking at job options and career opportunities. "Sometimes we need someone else to help us reflect on what we want to do next, and also what skills and talents we bring to the table," Koonce says. He adds that this role might also be filled by anyone who is a skilled listener and who has your best interests at heart.

Circle one:

In the next year, my highest career priority is to have more:

1. money
2. power
3. time
4. autonomy
5. productivity
6. creativity
7. other _____

Check this answer against your five-year goal. Give yourself a reality check by asking if the two aims are compatible. For instance, if you decided that you want to be in a more responsible job in your current line of work as a five-year goal, but said your highest priority in the next year is to have more time to yourself, that may be unrealistic. Or if you had a specific dream job in mind, does your priority for the upcoming year get you any closer to that job?

The exercises in this chapter are reminders for you to listen to your inner voice. Staying in touch with what you truly want—and making sure that your goals are in harmony, rather than working at cross-purposes—will do wonders for your success with feng shui. Remember, the clearer you are about your goals, the greater the probability that your practice of feng shui will get you where you want to go.

Fame
Fortune
Festivity
Red
Number: 9
Fire
Birds
Summer

Wealth
Fortune
Purple
Number: 4

Marriage
Partnerships
Motherhood
Yellow
Number: 2

Health
Family Life
Green
Number: 3
Wood
Dragon
Spring

Purity
Children
White
Number: 7
Metal
Tiger
Autumn

Knowledge
Intelligence
Scholarly
 Success
Turquoise
Number: 8

Travel and Interests
 Outside the Home
Benefactors
Fatherhood
Gray
Number: 6

Career
Business
Success
Death
Black
Number: I
Water
Tortoise
Winter

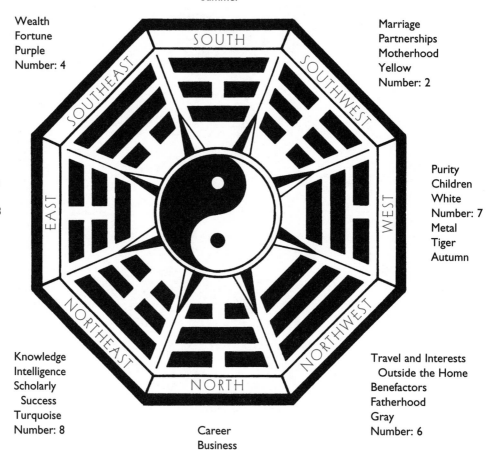

SOUTH

SOUTHEAST

SOUTHWEST

EAST

WEST

NORTHEAST

NORTHWEST

NORTH

3

BA-GUA BASICS

THE BA-GUA is one of the most powerful tools you have to create positive changes and transform your life with feng shui. The secret to using it is to take note of its characteristics and learn how to put them to clever use in achieving your goals.

The ba-gua is an octagonal chart (the Chinese term "ba-gua" means "eight-sided") that depicts the eight points of the compass. Each compass point governs a different aspect of life: career, knowledge, health, wealth, fame, marriage, children, and helpful people. These life aspects are influenced by certain universals: the five elements, colors, seasons, numbers, and the celestial animals. In the center of the ba-gua chart is the Taichi, the yin and yang sign enclosed in a circle. This is the symbol of completeness and a reminder that balance is essential.

COMPASS DIRECTIONS

WITH KNOWLEDGE of the compass directions, their characteristics, and their spheres of influence, you can make positive adjustments to remedy unfavorable situations and enhance the areas that will help achieve your goals.

SOUTH Fame (or your reputation), fortune, and festivity are governed by the south. This direction is considered so important and beneficial that the Chinese put south at the top of their compasses. You will always see feng shui charts with south positioned at the top. South's season is summer, its color is red, its number is 9, its element is fire, and the animal of the south is the phoenix. The mythical bird that never dies, the phoenix constantly re-creates itself, rising from the ashes of a fire that destroys it. The phoenix flies high and scans the landscape, collecting information; it is always on the cutting edge. With its great beauty, the phoenix creates intense excitement and burning inspiration. It represents our capacity for vision and creativity and can be especially important in the workplace. Like the phoenix rising from the ashes, from a blank piece of paper you might create a visionary business plan, a powerful direct-marketing letter, or a budget that positions your business for the future.

NORTH North governs career and business success and is one of the prime directions for achieving career goals. North's season is winter, its color is black, its element is water, its number is 1, and its animal is the tortoise. With its strong protective shell, the tortoise is characterized by stability, security, and longevity. The proper place for the turtle is behind you, where it frees you from the fear of attack from the rear.

EAST This direction governs health, growth, and family life. Its season is spring, its colors are green and light blue. The element is wood, the number is 3, and the animal is the powerful and inspirational dragon. Like the phoenix, the dragon is far-sighted and possesses a spiritual quality. While the quick-flying phoenix gathers information, the dragon receives and ponders it, making critical decisions. Known for its wisdom, the dragon is extremely powerful.

WEST   Children, children's luck, joyousness, and creativity are governed by the west. Its season is autumn, its color is white, its element is metal, its number is 7, and its animal is the fierce white tiger. A powerful and sometimes dangerous creature, the tiger can also be a wonderful protector. Just as it is constantly on the alert for danger, the tiger is capable of suddenly turning dangerous if it's not carefully controlled. In fact, the tiger represents the possibility for violence within human nature. But a well-controlled tiger could be your best friend as you stalk into your next budgeting session!

SOUTHEAST   Although half the compass points of the ba-gua influence wealth in some way, the southeast is the most powerful and most directly associated with riches. Perhaps this goes back to the earliest days of China trading with her Southeast Asian coastal partners. The number 4 and the color purple (associated with luxury) correspond to this direction.

SOUTHWEST   This compass direction governs relationships, marriage, partnerships, and motherhood. Activate this sector if you are interested in acquiring a business partner or strengthening any business relationship. Southwest's color is yellow and its number is 2—as in pairs. Earth is the element.

NORTHEAST   Want to increase your knowledge base? Improve your focus, concentration, and intellectual abilities? Turn to this direction for help. The green of growth and blue of lofty aspirations combine to make turquoise the operative color in this direction. The number 8 corresponds to the northeast. In Chinese the word for eight sounds like the word for prosperity, which is considered very lucky.

NORTHWEST   If you're attracted by far-flung places and interests that take you far from the domestic scene, cultivate the northwest area of your office. If you are hoping to expand your business beyond your own city, possibly taking it national or global, put special feng shui enhancements in the northwest area of your office. This direction also governs fatherhood, benefactors, mentors, and other people who may be of help to you. Its color is gray and its number is 6.

ELEMENTS

ACCORDING TO Chinese philosophy, the entire universe is made up of the five fundamental elements (fire, water, wood, metal, earth). These five represent the power of nature, its intricate interdependence, and its delicate balance. The agrarian Chinese who first took note of feng shui understood this, as do contemporary workers who depend on nature for the success of their enterprise. But most of us who work in urban and suburban environments tend to forget about this powerful force and can wind up feeling out of balance with the universe. This usually registers only at an unconscious level, making us feel uneasy, dissatisfied, helpless, or frustrated. When we consciously deploy the five elements in our feng shui designs, we get back in balance and begin to feel stronger and more in control.

Understanding a bit about how the five elements interact will make you a more skilled feng shui practitioner. Mixing, separating, and arranging the various elements at appropriate compass points is one of the basic methods of improving or repairing the feng shui of your office or home.

CREATIVE AND DESTRUCTIVE CYCLES

THE ELEMENTS interact in either a creative or a destructive cycle, and the way you use them in your office or work space will affect the success of all your endeavors.

In the creative cycle: Burning wood feeds fire; fire produces

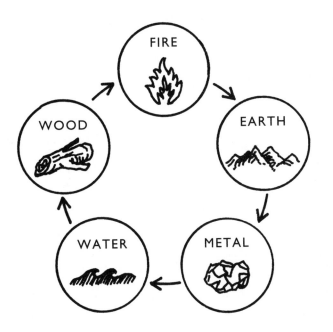

Creative cycle

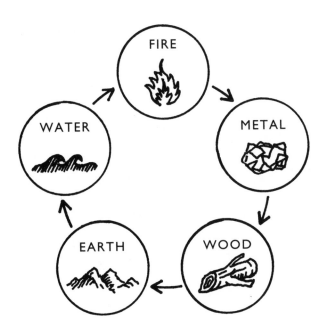

Destructive cycle

earth from its ashes; earth produces ore (metal), which creates water from condensation on its surface; water in turn nourishes plants and trees, creating wood.

In the destructive cycle: Water puts out fire, fire melts metal, metal cuts wood, wood takes nourishment out of the earth, earth muddies water.

No element is destructive in itself. In fact, all five are vital to your environment. The cycles become important when fine-tuning your surroundings to ensure that you aren't working against yourself with destructive placement.

For example, you want to avoid putting an aquarium on a south wall. Fire is the element of the south, and the water would douse the fire's effectiveness. Similarly, don't put a clay pot or a decoration featuring the color brown in the north area of your office, because north is ruled by water. This earth element may muddy your chances for career or business success.

ELEMENTS IN ACTION

HERE ARE daily, commonplace manifestations of the five elements and their colors:

Elements	Objects	Colors
Fire	Lighting, fireplaces, candles	Red
Wood	Plants, wooden furniture	Blue and green
Earth	Brick, tile, terra-cotta, stucco, stones, rocks, sand	Yellow and earthen shades

Elements	Objects	Colors
Metal	File cabinets, computers, fax machines, wrought iron, silver or gold picture frames	White and very light pastel tones
Water	Aquariums, sinks, toilets, reflective surfaces like mirrors, glass, and crystals	Black (the deeper the water, the blacker it is)

4

DESK FOR SUCCESS

THINK OF your desk as the heart of your office, the central staging area for your career. In the practice of feng shui, the position of your desk is crucial to determining the quality of your life—third in overall importance only to the bed you sleep in and the stove on which you cook your meals. The placement of your bed and stove influence many aspects of your personal life, from health and happiness to success and prosperity, while the placement of your desk is critical to the happiness, success, and prosperity you enjoy in your professional life.

Your desk is your domain, the center of your power, the place where you think, write, make important phone calls and critical decisions. It is the launching pad for your career and should be treated with the utmost respect. Its location can directly affect your success.

The attention you devote to your desk can result in huge boosts to your professional life. Its carefully arranged surface can increase your chances for promotion; and, most important, where your desk sits in the room can make or break your place in the business world. This applies whether you work in a corporate office or run a business from a corner of your living room.

KEEP YOUR
EYE ON
THE DOOR

THE GOLDEN rule in determining optimal desk placement is simple: When seated behind your desk, you must always be able to see the door. If your personal office space has no door (if you work in a cubicle or in an area of a large room), sit so that you can see the room's entrance or the entrance to your work space. If there is more than one door, keep the most frequently used one in your line of sight.

When you habitually face away from the door while seated at your desk:

- You'll always be surprised by people entering your office and (worse!) by the things they tell you.
- Because your back is exposed, you may be the victim of back-stabbing and dangerous office politics. This can put your job in jeopardy without your even realizing it.
- Even if you're the most easygoing person in the world, you can become paranoid in this situation and your colleagues *will* notice.

If you can't arrange your seating to face the entrance, hang a mirror over your desk to give you a "rear view" from your seat.

BE
COMMANDING

PLACE YOUR desk far enough inside the room so you have as much of the room in view as possible. This is the commanding position. If you are too near the door (and keeping your eye on it), most of the room will be out of your sight. What you cannot see, you cannot control. This is not to say you must be looking around the room constantly, but you should be able to see the area you work in with a quick glance. With this visual command you are more powerful because you're aware of your environment, quick to note any hint of change in the air, and quick to take action when necessary.

The most favorable position for your desk is diagonally across

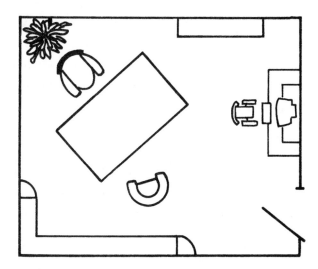

In the commanding position, you have maximum control over your office and the work you do

from the door with your back to a corner. In this ideal spot you will have the solid support of walls behind you. However pleasant and coveted windows are in a corporate setting, a window behind you means less backing for your ideas and authority.

BE PROTECTED

IF AT all possible, avoid placing your desk in direct line with the door. If you sit with your desk in the path of the door, you are vulnerable to drafts, noises, and countless other interruptions, and you are also unprotected from unwelcome surprises. The farther away from the door you sit, the more time you have to prepare for unexpected or unwanted visitors or any other difficult situations that present themselves suddenly.

The most serious threat to you in this position is sha chi, or poison arrows which dart through the door in an unbroken line. Because the negative effects of poison arrows vary widely, it's not possible to predict exactly what form they might have on you at work. You might suffer anything from lost paperwork to spilled coffee to clashes with your boss. Obviously some will be more serious than others. To avoid the problem altogether, either move your desk to the far corner from the door or put up a barrier between yourself and the door. A barrier on your desk might be a vase of flowers or a bushy desk plant, a file holder, or an in/out box. If none of these options is available to you, hang a mirror on the front of your desk facing the door so that it deflects poison arrows away from you.

CHOOSING YOUR DESK

MOST OF us are assigned desks and have little say in choosing them. But the design of your desk can make a difference, and there are ways to make any desk work without taking hammer and saw to it.

SHAPE Square, rectangular, or curving desks are fine. The one desk you'd do best to avoid is L-shaped. The "L" suggests incompleteness and also echoes the shape of a meat cleaver with the shorter end representing the blade. Constant exposure to the "blade" end of your L-shaped desk can undercut your authority, cut you off from communication with colleagues or your boss, cause chronic physical maladies, or cause any number of other serious effects.

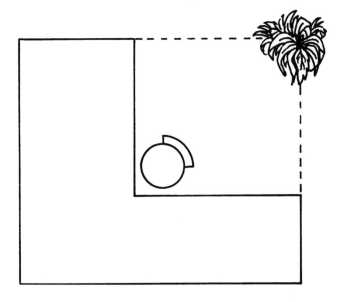

In reality, however, many desks are in precisely this L-shape because the "return," or shorter part, makes a convenient work surface, especially for those who use a PC or laptop regularly. The incompleteness of the L, along with its inauspicious meat cleaver shape, can be corrected by filling in that missing fourth corner. If you can do so without creating a hazard or obstruction, place a plant, wastebasket, floor lamp, or other solid object on the floor in the empty area.

If none of these remedies seems possible, increase the chi circulation around your work area. A strong, vibrant flow of chi around your desk will mitigate the ill effects of the unlucky cleaver shape and the incompleteness of the desk's structure. To boost the chi, try any of these enhancements: Find a small desk fan that will keep the chi circulating around your desk continually; suspend a crystal from the ceiling just above the empty spot to refract the light and attract more chi; or place a glass or crystal paperweight on the end of the desk closest to the "missing part." The crystal or glass object will catch the light, refracting it and sending chi into beneficial patterns around your desk.

DESK SIZE   Proportion is important in feng shui. Your desk should be large enough to allow you to work comfortably, but not so big that it overpowers the size of your office. Furniture that's too large to fit comfortably in a room will block chi circulation, slowing it down and causing it to stagnate. An office with slow or blocked chi will definitely hamper the ideas and creative ability of its occupant. Even worse, working in a room with motionless chi can cause your entire career to become sluggish.

The most important consideration in desk size is that each desk should represent the relative importance (or power) of each person in the organization. You may be thrilled to have a king-sized desk. But if your boss's desk is smaller than yours, the organization's hierarchy will be out of balance and the entire business will suffer from this lack of proper proportion.

Just as your desk must be sized proportionally to your manager's, it should be sized properly for you. A desk should be large enough to reflect the importance and power of its occupant, but not so big that it dwarfs its owner. Jamie Tarses, president of ABC Entertainment, is a case in point. She was the victim of a power play that seriously threatened her position because many of her superiors and colleagues believed her job was "too big" for her. Not coincidentally, a *New York Times* photo of Tarses at her desk shows her dwarfed by its huge blond surface. The desk also appears to be an inefficient work surface because most objects on it are out of her reach — just as many aspects of her job were judged to be by top executives at ABC.

MATERIAL   Once you have positioned your desk properly, take note of where it falls on the compass to see if you can put the elements to work for you. If proper placement allows, you may also reap benefits by matching the elements of your desk to the compass area in which it stands. Placing your wood desk in the eastern sector of the room will encourage growth, for example; moving your metal desk to the western part of your office will help jump-start your creative thinking.

A warning: Don't go out of your way to put your desk in a particular sector of the compass unless its position there works with the rules of desk placement. Where your desk is in the office is much more important than where it is on the compass.

Don't be concerned, for example, if rules of placement demand that your metal desk must stand by the east wall of your office. It's true that this arrangement can encourage a destructive cycle of elements, with the metal of the desk cutting into your chances for health and growth as represented by the east. But you can remedy this situation by putting the creative cycle to work. (Remember, it's all about balance!) Add water—perhaps a fish tank, a photograph of the ocean, or something blue—to your desk area to counterbalance the metal and any problems it may cause. In the creative cycle, the water element will nourish the wood that's represented by the east—and your endeavors at your desk.

ARE YOU one of those people who stacks papers, files, books, and magazines on and around your desk, with the vague notion that somehow, someday, you'll look them over and deal with them? You can't have an orderly thought process—or a creative one—if you are constantly surrounded by "stuff." And you won't reap the benefits of productive chi flow if all those stacks, piles, files, and so forth are blocking its path.

If a messy office robs you of energy and concentration because your mind is constantly distracted by the mess, you need to clean up your desk and any cluttered areas around it. In her book *Taming the Paper Tiger*, organizational guru Barbara Hemphill puts it this way: "A cluttered desk indicates a pattern of postponed decisions."

It's very difficult to pay attention to the project you're working on if the distractions of pending decisions constantly compete for your attention. You may think you can look past them, but you will be surprised at the boost you get from removing these obstacles and allowing your subconscious to relax and focus on the topic at hand. And of course, you'll have the additional bonus of smooth and steady chi flow moving around you in a life-enhancing way.

Begin to think of the establishment of order on your desk as one of the most important elements to achieving success and prosperity. This harks back to a basic feng shui principle: When you control your environment in a positive way, you encourage good chi flow, which in turn has a beneficial effect on all areas of your life.

DESK CLUTTER: WHY IT'S BAD AND WHAT TO DO ABOUT IT

Human resources director Jane Sefret, who works for a large health care organization, always held reasonably good jobs within her field, but worried about her history of frequent job changes. She found herself seeking new employment every two to three years. Since she knew she was competent and responsible, she was puzzled by the fact that whenever her employer had a reorganization or layoff (and this happened frequently in the 1980s) she was among the first to be let go.

After talking with a friend who is a feng shui practitioner, Jane realized that her frequent layoffs may have been caused in part by the way she'd always arranged her office and located her desk. She chose to sit near the door, thinking she would be more accessible to her staff. But to compensate for sitting so close to the door, where she was easily distracted, Jane *also* used to turn her desk away from the entrance. As it turned out, she had three strikes against her every place she worked. Sitting too close to the door made her less powerful; being in direct line with the door allowed sha chi (poison arrows) to attack her. And most important, having her back to the office door left her vulnerable to office politics and kept her out of the loop when important decisions were being made.

On the advice of her feng shui practitioner, Jane made a fairly simple change in her office layout, moving her desk so she faced the door and was sitting diagonally away from the entrance. She has been in her current job for five years now and was recently put in charge of a mentoring program for new employees. One of the first things she does is help them position their desks.

SPEND JUST one half hour today going through the stacks of paper on your desk. File or discard as much as you can. But only spend one half hour doing this and don't let yourself be overwhelmed by the task: Tomorrow is another day. Then spend half an hour policing the file boxes and other "floor clutter," ruthlessly throwing away what you don't need or use. The following day, spend another half hour, and so on, until you've whittled down the piles. Using this method, it probably won't take you more than a week to make your way through the clutter. And taking it in half-hour sessions will keep you from being overwhelmed by the job. Doing it in smaller time increments will also keep you from getting behind on the more immediate tasks of your work day.

So how do you decide what to leave on top of your desk?

This is, of course, a personal decision. But the rule of thumb from office organization experts is:

- Items you use daily belong on your desk. Your computer, message pad, pens, Rolodex, reference manuals, and diskette files can stay, along with anything else that is part of your daily work routine.
- Other items you use less often or don't need to have directly in front of you, such as a stapler, Scotch tape, paper clips, or Kleenex, can go inside your desk drawer.
- Don't store supplies in your desk. That is, keep no more than a few extra pens and one scratch pad in there. Put the box of pens and the bulk of spare pads, stationery, extra rolls of tape, and boxes of staples in the cabinet or credenza.
- By the same token, don't put things where they're hard to reach. For example, you shouldn't have to move a stack of file folders and open a box to get your letterhead stationery.
- Keep only one project at a time on your desk. File other folders and papers until you are working on those projects.
- Don't pay household bills at your office desk, or keep catalogs,

TAKING ACTION

vacation brochures, or other personal items out where you can be distracted by them. This is especially important if you work from home, where the temptation to blend business and personal paperwork will be strong.

· If you're worried that you'll regret throwing something away, get yourself a "hold" trash receptacle. Empty it only every few weeks. That way you can retrieve something if you decide you need it. But in the meantime, these papers are not cluttering up your desk.

Professional organizer Ilise Benun suggests you ask these questions about each piece of paper you file or throw away.

· Do I need this? Why?
· What's the next step?
· When will I need this?
· Where would I look for it? (Not "Where should I put it?")

Once you've controlled the clutter on your desk, you have literally cleared the air. Potent, positive chi can now flow freely around you, giving you more energy, inspiration, and power. As an added bonus, you'll be able to find what you're looking for easily. The result will be significantly less frustration and significantly more creativity and productivity for you.

Now that you've cleared extraneous files, paperwork, and just plain old junk off your desk, you're ready for the next step using the ba-gua and its elements to create a variety of feng shui enhancements on your desktop.

THE BA-GUA AND YOUR DESKTOP

THE BA-GUA chart can be superimposed on any surface (from an entire building or floor plan to a countertop or table). While the ba-gua can be used in your office as a whole, think of your desk as a miniature environment, to be analyzed and enhanced with the help of the chart.

You are about to turn your desktop into a work of art that symbolizes your dreams and enables you to work toward them with the practice of feng shui. Just as the clutter you used to have on your desk spoke to you in a negative way, the enhancements you are about to create will constantly speak to you. But they will say positive, career-enhancing things! And they will look lovely, soothing, and inspiring to you at the same time.

Get out your compass to see where north and south are in relation to your desktop. Once you've located these, turn to the ba-gua chart on page 22 and note where the eight life areas are in relation to your desktop.

Now you know which parts of your desk correspond to your special goals and aspirations. Spend some time reflecting on your two highest priorities from chapter 2. Remember not to get carried away working on too many goals at once. While thinking clearly about your goals, decide where you'd like to place special objects. These unique items will focus the power of feng shui on the areas most important to you.

A special object can be something you acquire especially to be used as a feng shui enhancement, say a small ebony tortoise or a crystal paperweight. But your own personal items, the things you keep on and around your desk, will also be very potent feng shui enhancements. Family photos in wood or metal frames, bookends, sculptures, paperweights, "found art" such as stones or sea shells, professional memorabilia such as certificates, plaques, trophies—anything you enjoy looking at or have a strong personal attachment to—can be used to great effect in turning the surface of your desk into a working ba-gua environment.

For example, let's say your desk sits so that you face south. That means the surface directly opposite you corresponds to the southern area of the ba-gua and governs fame and fortune. But fame needn't mean instant celebrity. Not everyone is interested in achieving the kind of attention Andy Warhol was thinking of when he ominously predicted that we'd all get fifteen minutes of fame. Many people would prefer to be recognized for their talent or accomplishments, to get new clients from word-of-mouth recommendations, or to be interviewed on television or radio about their special area of expertise. If you have your eye on a promotion or special assignment, you might want to encourage a "buzz" about yourself to increase your chances. These are just a few of the positive occurrences you may have in mind when you enhance the "fame" area of your desk or office.

To create an enhancement in the fame sector of your desk, choose something red because it is the color of the south. Or place an attractive lamp, representing fire, the south's element, in this area of your desk. You may even choose to put an important picture, award, or diploma—something that reminds you of your accomplishments or good reputation—in that spot. It should be framed attractively, of course. Consider a red mat or frame.

The southwest is the relationships, partnerships, and love area. If one of your top goals is to get along better with co-workers, improve your rapport with your boss, or find a partner for a business venture you have in mind, create enhancements corresponding to this direction. Use the color yellow and the number 2 on this part of your desktop in any ways that appeal to you. A vase with two yellow tulips would be lovely, but you can even use something as basic as a pair of standard number 2 pencils to enhance your prospects.

The west is the children's area, which represents not only children, but your inner child and all your creative powers. Enhance these powers with a metal or white item, such as a silver or chrome holder for your pens and pencils. Try to make it something directly symbolic or reminiscent of your creativity. It could even be a special painting or photograph that you (or one of your children) have made. To take advantage of the element as well as the color, put something your child has created in a white metal frame.

The northwest governs travel and helpful people (mentors, for example). Debra Baer, a journalist I know, keeps her appointment book in this spot because she's hoping for more national and international writing assignments. So far, she has managed a trip to Italy for a newspaper article on famous stone carvers in the village of Pietrasanta. You can enhance the travel aspect of the northwest with anything travel-related (like a souvenir or postcard), or your address book and appointment calendar—especially good if they're gray. To encourage mentor relationships, place a photograph of an important person who has helped or inspired you in the northwest. This is a great place to put a quote from one of your heroes or mentors. A mathematician friend who admires Archimedes had his quote "Give me a place to stand and I can move the world" written out in beautiful calligraphy, framed in matte silver (gray), and set on the northwest corner of his desk. I keep my telephone there to increase the number of considerate and well-meaning people who call me.

If you picture yourself within the octagonal sphere of the ba-gua and you face south, then directly behind you would be north, your career and business success area. If you have a bookcase, table, or credenza behind your desk chair, you have a perfect place to create any number of feng shui enhancements tailored to business success. Black, the color corresponding to the north, is correct even in the most conservative business environments. A black tortoise would be especially appropriate, perhaps a small ebony stone figurine. He is the animal of the north and can be an excellent protector, keeping watch and defending you from attacks from the rear. But any single black item you choose would work well in this area. If you don't have a table or other surface to put things on, by all means frame a beautiful black-and-white photograph and hang it on the north wall.

The northeast is your knowledge and intelligence area, symbolized by the color turquoise. If you have a meaningful object in this color, this is the place to put it. But the northeast section of your desk can also be a practical place to locate your reference books, materials for a current project, or anything you're working on that requires special knowledge or especially heavy mental lifting. This is also the spot for anything which represents newly acquired knowledge or self-cultivation. Have you studied a new language lately? joined an investment group? learned how to navigate the World Wide Web? Any such accomplishment can be symbolized in a way that's meaningful to you and placed in this area. The more you celebrate past accomplishments through feng shui enhancements, the more you create exciting possibilities for the future.

The eastern area of your desk is your health, growth, and family area, represented by wood and the color green. A plant is absolutely perfect in this space, bringing in green, wood, and growth all at once, along with a dose of good chi, which accompanies all living things. If your aspirations require growth, or if your health needs a boost, place a thriving green plant on the east side of your desk or on the floor next to it. Or if you really want to do something dramatic, choose the dragon, the most important celestial animal in feng shui. If you can locate a low-key dragon symbol to place in the eastern area of your desk, you will be inviting the power and wisdom of this creature into your office to guide you every day.

If you want to get a raise, generate more cash flow, save or raise money for a special purpose, or if you have any specific financial goal, then concentrate on the southeast (wealth) area of your desk. And if wealth or empowerment are at the top of your list, find the perfect red or purple item for the southeast sector. Since the number 4 correlates with this direction, a small bouquet of four stems of your favorite red or purple flower (tulips, irises, carnations, roses) would fit the bill beautifully. If flowers are not practical, put an item that is precious, either in terms of its cost or its meaning to you, in this spot.

A crystal paperweight will draw more chi to the area, a special coin, or a red or purple box for paper clips, note paper, or spare change are all good choices. A red or purple frame with a picture that

symbolizes your goal will work on several levels, giving you direct enhancement while it reminds you to keep your "reward" in mind.

Keep it simple when you do the ba-gua enhancements. They
shouldn't take up much room on your desk; if an enhancement is in
your way or impractical for any reason, don't use it. If you can't con-
veniently put special items on your desk, don't worry. In coming
chapters you'll find other opportunities to create practical yet powerful feng shui enhancements.

CUBICLE TO CORNER SUITE— GOOD FENG SHUI FOR EVERY WORK SPACE

NO MATTER where you work—in a cramped cubicle or spacious corner office, at a cash register, drive-up window, or nurses' station—you can create an environment that will enhance your natural gifts and propel you toward success in your chosen field.

You may work in a setting you didn't have a hand in designing; perhaps you don't feel comfortable because it seems crowded, depressing, or just not suited to your needs. Aside from coping with the strictly practical considerations of a badly arranged work area, you are also struggling against bad feng shui. If you find your surroundings unpleasant, it's certain that the feng shui is bad, and just as certain that you won't be functioning at your peak performance level.

No matter where you work, or how strict your employer's policies, there are always ways to raise the level of chi and create a sense of balance and harmony in your surroundings. When you practice feng shui at work, you take an active role in controlling your own destiny—and guiding your career.

OUTSIDE
THE BUILDING

TO ASSESS the overall feng shui of your workplace, step outside the building and have a look around to check the general quality of the site's feng shui. Give your workplace high marks if it is in an area with other successful businesses, because their success is itself an indication of good feng shui. Put more marks in the plus column if there are trees around the building and a fountain nearby or in the lobby. Trees, water, and the energy from other successful businesses will all contribute to good feng shui for your workplace. But you should also look carefully for sources of sha chi or poison arrows. Specifically, inspect your building for these four potential problems.

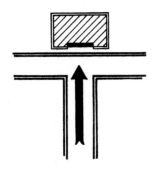

1. Are you located at a street's dead end or at the juncture of a T-intersection?

This is bad feng shui because sha chi will shoot forcefully along the narrow street and slice into your building, creating misfortune, illness, or business problems for those inside. You can block the sha by building a retaining wall or planting shrubs or hedges. If this isn't possible, put a small unobtrusive mirror high up on the outside of the building to deflect the sha.

2. Do telephone poles, streetlights, or the sharp angles of nearby buildings direct poison arrows toward yours?

Assuming you don't have the option of actually blocking these dangerous angles with walls or trees, do your best to locate your own office away from the part of the building that takes the brunt of the sha chi. Your best bet is to use the same measure suggested above: Put a small mirror on the outside of the building to deflect the arrows.

3. Do extremely tall buildings loom over the one you work in?

Tall buildings that dwarf yours can block the chi and good spirit surrounding it. Is it possible to create a rooftop garden with trees and tall plants? The garden doesn't have to reach as high as surrounding buildings; it will simply attract an abundance of healthy chi from the

The practice of hanging mirrors on the façades of buildings is extremely common in Hong Kong and in Chinese business districts in the United States. You can see this for yourself when you stroll through most Chinese business communities. Next time you're in one, look high up on the exterior of the buildings, close to the roof. Frequently you will see small octagonal mirrors glinting above. Next, look across from the mirror to see if you can locate the reason for it. Often you will see a telephone pole, streetlight, or jutting corner shooting poison arrows toward the building in question.

atmosphere and keep it moving around your building. If rooftop planting isn't practical, make certain you have plenty of clear light in your own office, either from windows or lamps, and a furniture arrangement that allows chi to circulate freely.

4. What is the shape of your building?

Just as with your desk, the most auspicious configuration for a building is square, rectangle, or—best of all—gently curving. It's no coincidence that Tung Chee-hwa, the new governor general of Hong Kong, chose the semicircular Asia Pacific Finance Center for the site of his office. An L-shaped office or building is inauspicious because the shape suggests something is missing—possibly revenues on your bottom line. You can correct this unlucky shape by "filling in" the missing corner. If you have permission, place a plant, pole, light, large decorative stone, or any other reasonably solid object in the empty area to represent that fourth corner. If you can't make such an adjustment to the outside of the building, remedy the situation with a mirror at the end of the L-shape, reflecting and essentially creating the missing part. This will draw the area into the main part of the room or building. You will then be working in a "whole" place with more secure financial prospects.

OFFICE
LOCATION

IF YOU have the luxury of locating your office anywhere you choose in the building, use the ba-gua chart to help you select the prime location for achieving your ambitions. For example, if your goal is to be more creative in your work, an office on the west side of the building would place you in the area that most strongly governs creativity. If you are doing research, computer programming, or other tasks that draw upon strong mathematics, academic, or scholarly talents, choose an office in the northeastern part of the building because the northeast has these cerebral pursuits in its sphere.

Tung Chee-hwa, who became the first Chinese governor general of Hong Kong when 150 years of British colonial rule ended July 1, 1997, is a great believer in feng shui. In fact, Tung declined to move into the existing governor general's office and residence because he felt the feng shui of the building was poor. Among other things, he noted downward arrows on an adjacent building that seemed to direct poison arrows right at the governor general's office. Tung hired his own feng shui master to analyze the offices he chose for himself in the Asia Pacific Finance Center. "Only after the feng shui expert nods his head to a place do I feel comfortable," said Tung.

THE MANAGER'S
OFFICE

ONE OF the most important considerations for the success and financial stability of any business is the location of the manager's office: It should be as far as possible from the entrance to the building. This is the same principle governing the placement of a desk in an office: the farther from the entrance, the greater the power. When there are many desks in one office, the person seated farthest from the entrance of the room will be the one with the most power. The person in this position has a commanding view of the room and can control the activities that go on in it as well as the people who work there. He or she should be the highest-ranking manager. If a subordinate sits in this position, everyone may suffer from power struggles.

Aside from the question of sheer power, when the person responsible for the "big picture" of a business sits too close to the entrance, he or she can be distracted by the minutiae of daily business. As much distance as possible from the front door ensures that the boss won't be swamped by petty details that interfere with strategic issues and long-range planning. With the perspective and serenity that a secluded office provides, the manager will have maximum control over the operation and sharp decision-making ability. This distance from the entrance also means the manager's authority will be respected because he or she is in command of the building.

LONG, NARROW corridors can encourage chi to move rapidly and harshly, bringing the ill effects of sha to those in its path and especially to anyone whose office is at the very end of the passage. If your building has such hallways, keep them well lit, add plants if there is room, and if you suspect sha chi is causing problems, hang a mirror on the walls (or exterior of doors) at either end of the corridor. Typical difficulties caused by sha can range from minor health problems among workers to constant foul-ups and confusion in business transactions.

HALLWAYS

DOORS THAT open directly opposite one another can create rivalry, arguments, grudges, and general bad feelings between the people who occupy the opposing offices. You can't do much about the placement of the doors, but you can increase the amount of healthy chi around the doorways and mitigate the problem with a green plant near each office entrance. It also helps to leave the doors open and have regular meetings between the occupants. Some businesses hang small crystals above each door to capture good chi and send it swirling in positive patterns.

FACING DOORWAYS

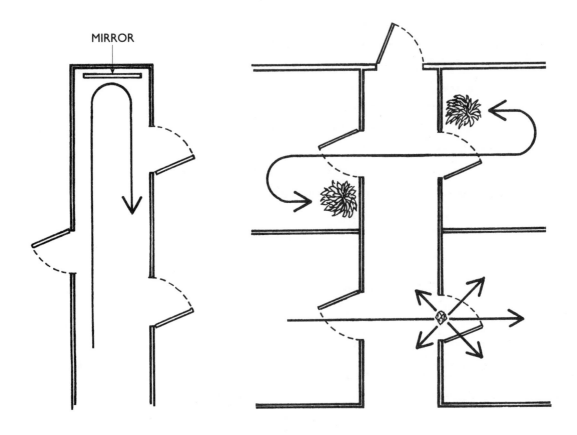

MIRROR

STAIRCASES

STAIRS OR escalators in the direct path of the entrance to a building or the door to an office are highly inauspicious. Chi travels rapidly on staircases and will quickly be drawn down the stairs and out of the building or room, taking good fortune with it. To remedy this, hang a mirror on the landing to reflect the chi and keep it from running out the door. Similarly, if a staircase leads straight into a room, put a mirror on the staircase door, if possible, to direct chi back into the room. Failing that, a plant immediately inside or outside the door to the room will encourage chi to circulate before racing away.

WITHOUT A doubt, cubicles are efficient, squeezing the maximum number of "offices" into one large work space. But the sharp angles on all those boxy little squares make for very bad feng shui. It's not a coincidence that even outside feng shui circles, the cubicle environment is generally regarded as depressing and dehumanizing.

When you think of cubicles, Dilbert—that hapless, cubicle-bound character of the Scott Adams cartoon strip—quickly comes to mind. With his flying tie and earnest but futile attempts to make sense of his absurd corporate culture, Dilbert is the Everyman of today's workplace.

The ubiquitous cubicle is a ready symbol for what troubles many people about their working environment: It isolates without giving privacy and creates barriers without providing a sheltering space. For many, working in a cubicle means working in an alien and *alienating* environment. Intuitively you know you are in the presence of bad feng shui. The squared-off edges of the individual cubicle and the repeat square pattern in the larger room create sha that shoots poison arrows throughout the area. As followers of Dilbert's daily struggles know all too well, nothing goes right in that environment; few things

THE CUBICLE

DILBERT reprinted by permission of United Feature Syndicate, Inc.

ever turn out according to plan. What readers may not have realized is that Dilbert is at the mercy of the bad feng shui of his workplace!

An overhead view of an office with cubicles is reminiscent of a rat maze, symbolizing the way many people feel about working in a cubicle environment. This is a distinctly different environment from anything our predecessors encountered when they went off to toil in forests and fields not all that long ago. No wonder working in cubicles seems to lower employee morale at approximately the same rate it raises available office space.

Don't despair. If you work in a cubicle, there are steps you can take to bring balance, harmony, healthy chi, and good feng shui to your environment.

Chances are you cannot see the opening which passes for a door to your cubicle when you're seated. If you work with a computer all day, the first thing you should do is arrange your desk so you can at least glimpse the entrance while at your keyboard. If most of your day is spent poring over something other than a computer, set up your area so the place where you do most of your work allows you visual contact with the entrance.

If that's not possible, place a mirror in the direction you face so you can view the opening to your cubicle in its reflection. Depending on the size and style of the mirror you hang, it may also serve to visually open up the space you work in. The mirror will capture good chi and disperse it to your surroundings. Find an interesting mirror (it doesn't have to be large) with a frame that includes elements and colors you're using to achieve your goals.

Your choices are extremely varied: Figure out where you need to hang the mirror to get the door view. Which direction is that? Does it coincide with an important goal of yours? For example, if the mirror needs to hang on a south wall and if fame or heightened visibility within your company is your aim, choose an elaborately carved wooden frame painted red. The wood feeds fire, which is the element of the south, and the color red is exactly right for the direction that governs fame. Such an exotic mirror will also add a distinctive air to your "office" and you'll notice co-workers dropping by to soak up the positive ambiance. Spend some time looking at the ba-gua chart on page 22 and use your imagination (as well as your lunch hour) to find just the right framed mirror to be an attractive and strategic feng shui enhancement, no matter what your goal.

To get as much good chi as possible into your cubicle, take the same actions you would in a larger office. Put a plant on your desk or, if you have enough space, on the floor. This vibrant living thing will draw positive chi to the area while it enhances the appearance of your work station. If possible, put the plant in the east because that's the di-

Nancy Richards, photo editor for a children's cable television channel, found her cubicle so inhibiting and dehumanizing that she often wasn't able to do her best work. She also worried that when she did accomplish something significant, no one noticed anyway. We met at a party, and I suggested a variety of feng shui techniques for improving her surroundings. The "cure" that worked best for Nancy turned out to be a bright yellow pennant—a promotional item for one of the shows on her channel—hoisted above her cubicle. The banner caught enough draft from the air conditioning to waft softly, attracting good chi and counteracting the hard angles and poison arrows that had surrounded her. Yellow, the color of the southwest, gradually brought the warmth of relationships she felt were lacking in her isolated work space. Since individualizing her cubicle with this feng shui enhancement, Nancy reports feeling more comfortable and creative in her job and happier with her overall interactions at work.

rection with wood (plants) as its element. This way the plant will double as an enhancement for any goals you might be working toward having to do with health, growth, and new beginnings.

Don't be afraid to get creative. A few workers at America Online's large office building in Sterling, Virginia, have personalized their six-foot-high cubicle partitions by hanging "love beads" over the entrances. Some beads are made of wood, others plastic. With this sixties-style decorating touch they've brought color and movement, as well as greatly enhanced chi, to their working environments.

THE LARGE ROOM WITH MANY DESKS

WHEN YOU work in an open area with several desks, you may have no choice as to whether you face the door, nor will you likely have much control over your distance from it. Employ the usual feng shui precautions if you work in a situation like this. Use a mirror to see the door if you sit with your back to it. Use plants or mirrors to shield everyone in the room from poison arrows coming from the sharp corners of other desks and file cabinets. Space the desks so that narrow aisles don't create sha chi.

Remember that the manager's desk should be as far from the door to the room as possible. Everyone in the company benefits when the manager is seated far enough from the door to provide maximum command over the room. The health of the business—and the success of everyone who works there—requires that the manager be as effective as possible.

Avoid having employees' desks face one another directly in a large room. If possible, stagger them slightly just to break up the direct one-on-one effect. When that's not possible, be sure to put a small barrier—most ideal is a green plant—on the facing end of each desk. I have seen many offices in which seeming personality problems between employees really stemmed from the "relationship" of their desks.

Also, in a large room with many desks, it's important to use subtle colors rather than bright ones because vivid colors can tip the balance of yang in a large bustling room and make it unpleasant as well as unlucky to work in.

LOBBIES, FOYERS, waiting rooms, and receptionist desks should be given careful feng shui consideration because they set the tone for a person's entire experience on the premises. These areas should have good light and chi circulation as well as a mix of hard and soft surfaces and light and dark colors to keep yin and yang in balance. Above all, they should appear spacious and welcoming.

FIRST
IMPRESSIONS

No professional will do as much good for the client as one whose waiting or reception area has good feng shui. An accountant with a dark, chi-deprived waiting room will have fewer—and less trusting— clients than an equally competent professional whose lobby provides an upbeat and welcoming environment. Customers who wait in a lobby with good feng shui begin each accounting session with the confidence that comes from experiencing a balanced and harmonious atmosphere. They literally feel better about themselves and about their prospects for prosperity before they even sit down in the accountant's office.

All the fundamental feng shui principles apply in waiting rooms and reception areas. Here are the basics to keep in mind:

- Use soft colors and lighting to soothe visitors, but keep the chi moving with mirrors, ceiling fans, crystals, or living things such as plants or fish.
- Pay particular attention to ensuring that the feng shui is as good for the people who work there as it is for those who visit. The receptionist's desk should be as uncluttered and serene looking as the company president's. All other principles of feng shui

should also apply. Make sure to fill in the missing piece of an L-shaped desk, for example. After all, the appearance of the receptionist's desk and the morale of the receptionist tell clients something important about the overall condition of the business.

· Camouflage sharp corners with plants to soften the effects of poison arrows, as well as to welcome and cheer those who enter the area.

Dr. Irv Cohen, a Fargo, North Dakota, surgeon with excellent qualifications and a friendly, compassionate manner, was puzzled because his practice was dwindling. At his wife's suggestion, Dr. Cohen hired an interior designer with a feng shui background to redecorate his suite of offices. The designer had no trouble locating the source of Dr. Cohen's declining practice. The waiting room was small and gloomy, with furniture that somehow didn't look right in the space. Patients who spent any time at all in the waiting room arrived in Dr. Cohen's office feeling chilly and nervous, with very low energy. No matter how compassionate and competent Dr. Cohen's techniques were, his patients came away from the visit feeling ill at ease and less healthy than when they'd arrived. After Dr. Cohen repainted the walls in a soft peach (a color of the southwest sector chosen to enhance the doctor's relationships with his patients and also to brighten the room), hung a mirror (to circulate chi as well as enlarge the appearance of the room), rearranged the furniture to allow gentle meandering chi patterns, and changed the lighting so that it was intimate without being gloomy, his practice began to flourish.

THE HUMBLE, often taken-for-granted coffee room or office kitchen is actually a very important space in terms of overall harmony and balance at work.

 If your office pantry has a stove and sink, you must treat this area like a kitchen, paying special attention to the room's two powerful but clashing elements: fire, which is yang, and water, which is yin. Keep one from overwhelming the other by avoiding the color red (which will enhance fire) or black (which amplifies the element water) in the decor.

 If a stove, coffee machine, or microwave (all representing fire) is right next to the sink, the proximity of the conflicting elements will drastically upset the yin/yang balance. Luckily, this is easy to fix by placing something metal or wood as a buffer between them. A can of coffee or tin of cookies, a plant or wooden box, should be easy to keep on the counter. White, a symbol of purity, is always a good color for a kitchen or any area where food is prepared or eaten.

 In the hierarchy of feng shui, the placement of the stove comes second in importance after the bed, even before the desk. If your office kitchen has a traditional stove, make sure a person standing at it can see the door to the room. If not, hang a mirror over the stove.

 The mirror can serve two purposes if it also reflects the number of burners on the stove. The burners, and their role in cooking food and providing the major portion of most meals, symbolize the business's income potential. Their mirrored reflection will double this potential. For this reason it's essential to keep the stove clean and all burners working. The heat and energy passing through the stove jets will keep the business's financial prospects from going cold.

 Since coffee rooms are common areas, they are the "morale centers" of many workplaces. If good feng shui is neglected here, low productivity, bickering, and ill will among employees may result.

 Every personal item that gets tacked on the bulletin board or left behind in the room has its own kind of energy, or chi. Try to keep this

COFFEE ROOMS

upbeat. Pictures of new babies, invitations to parties, announcements of professional and social gatherings, and certain jokes all contribute to a positive mood and create a healthy pulse of chi in the room. Anonymous complaints, snide notes about cleaning up, mean-spirited jokes, and any general trash or unclaimed personal items left around will inhibit the chi in the room and cause morale problems.

Often, coffee rooms have no windows, so keep the chi moving with good light, and perhaps a ceiling fan, mobile, or crystal suspended from the ceiling.

COPIER, FAX, FILE, AND SUPPLY ROOMS

ROOMS THAT house files, supplies, and the copier and the fax machine often have an overabundance of metal that you will want to balance with wood or earth elements. For excellent balance in your file or equipment room, hang a photograph, painting, or even a calendar depicting a pleasant nature scene with trees or mountains. In addition to balancing the elements, the outdoor scene will also introduce the gentle shapes of nature into the man-made environment of the room. Storing paper in or near the copier or fax machine will also help balance the metal with wood. As always, make sure there is good light and as much air circulation as possible.

THE HOME OFFICE

IF YOU are one of the eleven million plus Americans who work from home, you enjoy free rein in arranging the feng shui of your workplace. At the home office, as in any office, observe the feng shui principles.

- Encourage healthy chi flow
- Avoid sha chi in the form of poison arrows
- Take care to balance yin and yang
- Create special enhancements to help achieve your goals

In addition to these basics, there are a few special feng shui considerations if space limitations dictate putting the home office in a room that is already being used.

Sometimes just making space for a desk and minimal office equipment can throw off the feng shui balance in a household. Try to avoid crowding any one room. If you've set up the office in a small area, use mirrors to increase the sense of space. Look carefully at how the added office furniture changes the feng shui of the room. It may very likely require some feng shui adjustments once the office equipment has been put in place.

If your office area is part of your home kitchen, pay attention to the balance of elements, remembering that fire and water are part of your feng shui equation. Treat the kitchen in similar fashion to the coffee room described earlier. Working in the kitchen does give you the advantage of having fire (south/red/fame) and water (north/black/ career success) right there in the room. Create your enhancements by taking advantage of the presence of these powerful elements. (Just make sure you don't allow either element to overwhelm the room.)

For example, if your first priority is to make a name for yourself and expand your client list through word-of-mouth, put a small red decoration, even a single rose or picture of one, on or just above the stove. If your primary goal is to build up your capital, be sure to create enhancements around the sink (water = money); again, this could be something as simple as a photo or artwork featuring fish (for abundance), or a black turtle as a special water enhancement that connotes longevity and stability—two cherished ambitions of any new business!

When the home office invades your bedroom, you must be very careful. Avoid mixing these two areas of your life if at all possible; the office will bring too much energy into a room which is meant to be restful. A bedroom with good feng shui and an office with good feng shui contain very different kinds of chi, making the two essentially incompatible. An office calls for brisk, lively chi, while a well-balanced bedroom has healthy yet gently moving chi. What happens most often in these situations is that the stronger energy dominates, and the bedroom—and the sleep of its inhabitants—suffers as a result.

When putting an office in the bedroom is unavoidable, create as definite a barrier as possible between the two functions of the room. This is one circumstance where you will need more than a large floor plant. Here are a few suggestions:

- Invest in an attractive room divider to separate the office from the sleeping area
- Put an area rug on the floor to mark off the office
- Build a slightly raised platform for your desk

Any of these will encourage the two distinct chi patterns to move in their individual ways, allowing you to keep a high-energy chi flow in the office without disturbing the gentler chi flow needed for a good night's rest.

No matter where your business is located, decorate your office to appeal to the clients you want to attract, even if they never come to your office. When you do this, you are boosting the energy and greatly enhancing the prospects for your enterprise. You should also dress reasonably well when you work at home. Despite what some advertisements for home office technology would have us believe, spending the day unshowered and in your pajamas will not do much to enhance your personal chi or your professional appeal.

ON THE ROAD

WHEN YOU travel for business, you can create good feng shui as you go. In fact, it's important that you do. Leaving a familiar environment and going to a strange place can leave you feeling vulnerable, with weakened chi. The stress and strain of travel also depletes your chi.

Barbara Sternau started her interior decorating business at her home in Westchester County, New York, more than a decade ago. She was fortunate enough to have an unused room in which to set up her office, although she felt the space was a bit too cramped to be ideal. Nevertheless, she did everything possible to maximize the good feng shui potential that was there. An alcove in the knowledge area of the office troubled her because the natural flow of chi didn't circulate into this crucial sector. She hung a mirror on the setback wall, drawing chi into the recessed area. She was concerned about money, of course, so she put the part-time bookkeeper's desk and computer in the room's wealth area. Her own drafting desk went into the relationship corner because Barbara knows that relationships are key in her business. This all worked so well that a few years later Barbara achieved her primary goal—to expand her business enough so that she could move out of her home office and into a new (larger) location.

It's vital to do all you can to bring good feng shui with you and to arrange your unfamiliar surroundings so that you feel in control and powerful once again.

If you can, call ahead and request a room that faces south, north, east, or west—whichever direction would best suit your goals. (The room "faces" whichever direction has the window letting in the most light.) Pack one or two small enhancements to place along the windowed wall in a way that furthers your goal for the trip. If you'll be negotiating lucrative business contracts, for example, try to get a southeast facing room. When you arrive, purchase a simple enhancement for that area of the room (I always suggest four purple irises), or bring a significant picture including the color purple. These steps will put you in a position of considerable strength in financial negotiations because you've enhanced the southeast, which is the most powerful money area of the ba-gua chart.

If the desk in your hotel room is placed so that you are sitting with your back to the door, don't hesitate to drag it around to face the other direction. Sometimes hotel rooms have just a writing table rather than a formal desk; in that case all you need do to give yourself a view of the door is move the chair from one side of the table to the other.

And don't feel you must live with any unappealing art you find hanging on the walls when you check in (unless it's bolted to the wall, as is sometimes the case). Take down any negative or unpleasant images and slip them under the bed. Be sure to hang them up again before you leave so the management doesn't bill you for them!

Telecommunications consultant Rose Murray travels on business several times a year and has become adept at tailoring the feng shui of any hotel room to suit the needs of her trip. On one particularly delicate occasion, she needed to gain the trust of an important—and highly skeptical—potential client. Rose brought along a yellow damask tablecloth, a family heirloom, and draped this prized possession attractively over a dresser in the southwest corner of her suite. She purchased a pair of yellow tulips and placed them on the dresser as well. This feng shui enhancement was carefully arranged to promote a good business relationship and seems to have done the trick. Rose had a breakthrough in her talks with this executive and had signed him on as a client by the end of her business trip.

FENG SHUI AND THE BOTTOM LINE

CHECK BACK to your list of goals from chapter 2 and review your major objectives. If boosting your bottom line in any form—from getting a raise in salary to expanding your new business—was high on your list, read this chapter closely; it will give you detailed instructions to help you realize those dreams. Here you can blow up that desktop ba-gua (as discussed in chapter 4) to make use of your whole office. Take advantage of the freedom of working with a three-dimensional space.

The suggestions are made with a conservative corporate culture in mind. If you work in a more informal environment, by all means use your imagination and be as creative as possible in expanding on these ideas.

IF YOUR primary goals include

- gaining promotions
- landing specific jobs
- getting better contracts or more lucrative assignments

BUSINESS AND CAREER SUCCESS

use north with its colors and elements to achieve any goals that relate directly to your career.

Enhance the north area of your office with black, water, the number 1, and call upon that symbol of longevity and stability, the tortoise. A striking black-and-white Ansel Adams print featuring water would be a good choice here. If you can't hang artwork, you can create a very discreet feng shui enhancement with a small ebony tortoise on a credenza, bookshelf, or desktop situated on a north wall. Putting something metal, such as a piece of equipment, a sculpture, even a metal picture frame, in the north will accentuate your business acumen because in the creative cycle of elements, metal gives birth to water. Similarly, do not put anything earthen or symbolic of earth in the north because in the destructive cycle, earth dirties water; this will muddy your chances for career advancement.

FORTUNE AND FAME

IF YOUR hopes revolve around

- improving your reputation
- earning a high degree of respect for your authority
- making your name more familiar to clients or colleagues
- increasing visibility for yourself or your business regionally or nationally
- gaining publicity or notoriety
- getting a rapid influx of cash

then center your efforts on the south. There is a certain drama associated with gaining fame and fortune, so it makes sense that the colors and elements of the south are appropriately dramatic. Use vivid reds, symbols of fire, or any spectacular bird (remember this is the direction of the phoenix) to increase your chances for the blessings of this highly auspicious direction. Since 9 is south's number, you could hang a photo with nine birds (red cardinals are a possibility) on a south wall. But you don't need to use that number in all your enhancements. Any attractive red object, especially if it represents fire, like a candlestick, will work just fine. Even a single red rose in a bud vase will enhance your chances for fame and fortune. You can also take advantage of the creative cycle of elements by adding wood on a south wall. This will intensely stimulate the fame, fortune, and festivity in your life because south is the fire direction and wood feeds fire. Avoid the destructive cycle of the elements by keeping water away from your southern area, since water puts out fire and will dampen your chances for fame and fortune.

IF YOUR most important goals revolve around money in any of these forms

MONEY

- start-up capital for a new business
- improved cash flow
- wiser investment strategies
- better control of finances
- earning bonuses or big commissions

then focus your attention on the southeast, using the number 4 and the color purple as well as deep reds and pinks.

Of all the eight ba-gua compass points, the southeast is the one most unabashedly focused on the bottom line. If you have set your sights on money, use your imagination to create enhancements that will activate your southeast corner with deep, luxurious colors and the number 4. Flowers brighten the office, increase chi, and have the added benefit of making it easy to work in the color and number you need. But a word of caution here. You must do the footwork to clear up your finances before you can hope for help from feng shui. Four irises in the southeast corner of your office won't compensate for a chaotic checking account or bills that are overdue for payment (because you lost them!).

GROWTH AND HEALTH

IF YOU'RE primarily interested in any of these goals

- gaining new clients
- enlarging the business with new products or services
- adding staff or associates
- recovering from business setbacks and improving the "health" of the business

then look to the east, because that is the direction of growth and health.

The element of the east is wood, the color is green, the number is 3. The powerful, inspiring dragon is the celestial animal that keeps watch over this direction. Green plants are an obvious and very easy choice for activating your eastern sector. They incorporate the element, color, and spirit of the growth-oriented east. To bring as many enhancements as possible into play, try to group them in threes. If your work area isn't conducive to living greenery, silk plants are an acceptable option. Be sure to keep them dusted; if neglected they will become a negative influence. To use the creative cycle of elements in this area, add water or a representation of it because water nourishes wood and all growing things. By the same token, avoid using metal in this sector because metal (the element of the west) destroys wood, cutting into the blessings of the east in much the same way a metal ax cuts into a tree.

And one more note of caution about achieving your business goals through the use of feng shui. No feng shui enhancement will substitute for good customer service, smart marketing tactics, and overall good business practices. The enhancements are no more than supports or boosters for your own professional efforts.

WATER IS the most powerful symbol of money in feng shui, and it is said that the deeper the water, the greater the possible wealth. Moving water can also help attract and create good chi in addition to encouraging status and wealth for those who are blessed by its presence.

WATER, WATER EVERYWHERE

Just as with chi, the flow of water is critical in using water to your benefit. If water rushes too rapidly, it creates sha, or negative chi. Imagine your good luck racing away with the fast-moving water.

Polluted or algae-choked water is equally dangerous. Living or working near foul water will stagnate your chances for success in business and relationships and may cause health problems as well.

Although swimming pools and lakes don't have much natural flow to them, the natural movement added by the air—a pump in a pool or the wind on a well-positioned lake—creates very good feng shui as long as the water is healthy. (After all, "feng" means "wind" and "shui" means "water"!)

Fish tanks and aquariums are excellent for bringing success and prosperity to your office. The movement and flow of water in the fish tank symbolizes positive cash flow. The fish add to the power of the water because they are another symbol of abundance (there are always more fish in the sea!). Goldfish and koi are often found in Chinese ponds and fish tanks because their gold color further symbolizes money and is thought to attract it.

If you do put an aquarium in your office, be sure to keep the fish healthy, the tank clean, and the pump in good working order. No fish tank at all is better than one with murky water and sick and dying fish.

My friend and colleague Angi Ma Wong tells an impressive story of her own experience with fish tanks and feng shui. When the water pump broke on the saltwater aquarium in her busy office, she let it go for a few months. Her usually brisk business began to slow down somewhat, leaving Angi time to clean the large tank. She scrubbed out crystallized salt, replaced the magnet inside the motor, and restarted the motor with a strong, bubbly flow of water in the tank. She left the office for several hours and returned that evening to find ten messages on her voice mail, many of which resulted in media interviews and contracts for her intercultural consulting business.

Angi's story dramatically illustrates the importance and power of rapidly circulating water in activating the business and career aspects of life. As Angi put it, "By paying attention to the problems of my aquarium—a minienvironment of its own—I had jump-started my business life as well as the water pump."

Jacinta and Paul Porto, working parents of four small children in northern Virginia, learned firsthand about the power of fish tanks. After listening to the pleas of her children for pet fish, Jacinta bought a twenty-gallon aquarium and put it in the money area of their family room. One month later, the family won a Back to School Night raffle. Their prize was one year's free tuition to their children's school, which represented a huge windfall for them. Two months later, after the family's CD player broke (and they concluded it would be too expensive to repair), they won a church raffle, and this time the prize was a portable CD player! Jacinta and her husband, who both work for a paint and decorating company, are always experimenting with new feng shui enhancements, and they feel the tank has been a particular success for them.

Fountains are especially beneficial because the movement and splash of playing water encourages good chi flow. Increasingly, fountains can be found indoors, and not just in the elegant atriums of downtown office buildings. Garden stores feature fountains that are perfectly designed and scaled for office or home use. It's even possible nowadays to purchase desk fountains that will soothe you with gentle gurgling sounds while the water moves around, busily enhancing your wealth.

Corporate training coach and counselor Edith Berke was suffering through a sluggish time in her business. Her individual clients were dropping away and her corporate clients—the bread and butter of her practice—were not calling. Edith consulted her local feng shui practitioner, who suggested moving a beautiful black ceramic fountain from the back patio right into Edith's home office, where the floors are made of ceramic tile. Within two weeks of adding the color black and the element water to the north office wall, Edith had a lucrative contract with a brand-new corporate client.

It's no coincidence that dozens of office buildings in Hong Kong and an increasing number of skyscrapers in the United States have fountains in their lobbies.

If you aren't able to have a fish tank or fountain in your office or work space, you can obtain excellent feng shui results by using art that depicts water. Sailing ships on the ocean, waterfalls in Yosemite, rivers coursing through meadows, virtually anything that appeals to you aesthetically or emotionally and represents water, can improve your relationship with money if placed properly.

Hong Kong is a city of phenomenal wealth where it's not at all uncommon to see businessmen being chauffeured about town in their Rolls-Royce and Mercedes sedans. The people of Hong Kong credit the city's great affluence to its excellent feng shui location. Victoria Peak stands guard over the city, protecting it from behind, while the harbor in front attracts money. In this case, the water is both literally and symbolically the source of the city's wealth.

The citizens are certain that the city will continue to prosper now that Hong Kong has been handed over from British to Chinese rule, in part because the harbor is thought to be shaped like a "money bag" with a narrow opening so that wealth can come in but not flow out again. Also, many buildings facing the waterfront have been specifically designed by architects in conjunction with feng shui masters to look and act like magnets, pulling wealth from the water. It seems to be working, since the port bustles with shipping, exporting, and all manner of global business that brings glittering wealth to the city.

MIRRORS

MIRRORS CAN boost your bottom line because they symbolically double whatever they reflect, giving your assets twice their strength. Luckily, they're aesthetically appealing and also practical, so you can put them in any number of places. Here are some suggestions:

- Place a mirror beside the cash register to double your income
- If your reception area is small or cramped, hang a mirror there to double the space
- If you own a restaurant or other business where people gather, put a mirror on one wall to double the number of customers

Louise Perez works in a corporate travel agency in the Midwest. A few years ago she was frustrated because she felt blocked in her career path and was overdue for an increase in salary. Louise was ready to put feng shui to work on her career ambitions, but company policy did not allow her the option of fountains, fish tanks, or even personally chosen art to bring the element of water into her work space. Given these constraints, Louise had to be extremely resourceful and clever about the way she created a feng shui enhancement to help her achieve her goals. What she came up with was a "lake" made from a six-inch-diameter mirror placed flat on her desk. In the summer, she put tiny sailboats and even tinier little "flying fish" into the scene. In the winter, she put little felt dot fishing holes and toy fisherman on the lake to show that beneath its frozen surface, fish swam abundantly and water moved freely. Her clients loved the little pond and always got a kick out of seeing how she arranged it for each season. Gradually, Louise began to book more and more travel for the company. Soon she was the busiest and most popular agent on the floor and received a large bonus for hitting an ambitious target the company had set for new bookings. Louise was at the top of that bonus list for three years and the following year she was named associate vice president for travel.

She carefully polishes her little lake mirror and dusts her tiny fish regularly!

RELATIONSHIPS AT WORK

CREATING A balanced and harmonious environment with feng shui at home and at work can literally do wonders for your wealth, health, and success. But to get the most satisfaction from any of those benefits, you must enjoy good relationships. When you bring feng shui to bear on your personal interactions, you will see transformations in the way you respond to people and the way they react to you.

These transformations may be achieved in a variety of ways. With feng shui you can:

- develop your personal chi so that others will be drawn to you and will enjoy being in your presence—this will help you gain clients and build your business
- create an environment that can make people feel confident in your abilities and inclined to trust you and listen to your opinions
- learn how to put yourself in the command position no matter where you are conducting business so you will have authority in any environment

If your goals from chapter 2 include improved relationships, or increased authority, this section of the book will be especially important to you.

DEVELOPING PERSONAL CHI

IT IS possible to become a more authoritative presence at work, to maintain supportive and collegial relationships with co-workers, and encourage your boss to see you in a whole new light when you have robust personal chi.

People who seem to know who they are and who welcome others into their presence actually have a kind of power over people. Sometimes this power is pure charisma, sometimes it's the ability to persuade others to a way of thinking, and sometimes it's a strong authoritative quality that others respect. People with this special presence often excel in positions of leadership.

Your personal chi is the most important ingredient for improving relationships. When your individual chi is strong, you are alert, self-assured, and filled with energy. You are relaxed about who you are and are less likely to be judgmental or harsh in your perceptions of others. Most people can sense these qualities quickly and are naturally drawn to those who exhibit them.

SELF-AWARENESS IS KEY

KNOWING YOURSELF is vital to bringing your personal chi to its fullest possible potential. Make it a practice to have heart-to-heart talks with yourself (sometimes known as meditations) on a regular basis. These will help you cultivate your special strengths and zero in on areas you'd like to improve. Do the following exercise as often as you need, but at least every few months, to keep clear channels of communication between yourself and your inner self. The inner self is the core of your being and determines the quality of your personal chi. So listen to it carefully and speak to it kindly.

A GREAT way to clear and strengthen your personal chi is with daily breathing exercises. Many feng shui practitioners start their day with a simple inhaling and exhaling process that brings plenty of oxygen to the heart and brain and lots of brisk chi to the spirit.

BREATHING EXERCISES

Take a deep breath through your nose. Hold it for about three seconds. Then exhale slowly through your mouth with eight short breaths followed by a long breath.

As you repeat this a few times (don't make yourself dizzy), imagine filling yourself with bright and vibrant chi. Feel the chi entering your mind and spirit, preparing you for the day ahead and giving you the serenity, strength, and wisdom to handle all the day's challenges.

SET ASIDE about an hour to do the following exercise, which will help you develop valuable insights about yourself. In this exercise you will create a list of changes to make and actions to take.

MEDITATION

1. Sit in a quiet place and in a comfortable position (but don't lie down—you don't want to fall asleep!). Spend a few minutes doing the breathing exercise above to prepare your mind for the exercise ahead. Have a pencil and pad of paper handy to jot down your thoughts as you go.

2. Picture yourself arriving at work on an ordinary day. How do you feel? Full of anticipation? dread? anxiety? energy? anger? happiness? boredom? Jot down the emotion that most closely matches the first feeling that comes to your mind. Then ask yourself what evokes that feeling (good or bad) and jot that down quickly.

3. Next, imagine yourself going through a typical workday. What feeling predominates in different parts of your day and during interactions with different people? Do you feel powerful and competent? Confused and not in control? Write down those feelings and note the triggers to those emotions.

4. Reflect on the interactions you have with co-workers. Are you at ease with them? Do you have unfinished business or bad feelings with some? Write down any names that occur to you along with a one-word notation about your relationship.

5. Picture yourself in a meeting with a group of co-workers. What quality do you think you project? Do you have a sense of the way you're perceived by these colleagues? How do you feel about that? Is there anything you'd like to change about your own behavior?

6. Recall your most recent interactions with your immediate supervisor. What emotions dominate here? First, write down how you feel; next, jot down what you think your boss is feeling.

7. Give some thought to what motivates you most strongly in your career. Money? Power? Reputation? A sense of accomplishment? A desire to change the world or make something better? This time don't just write the first thing that comes to mind, especially if the word is "paycheck." That may or may not be the case. Think about it long enough to determine what gets you going and keeps you working even when you may be tired or discouraged.

8. Ask yourself what most needs to be changed at work. Jot down as many answers as come to mind.

9. Think about each change that needs to be made. Where should it start? Does the change involve relationships or interactions with your boss or colleagues? What can you do to begin the process? Write down any actions you could take to initiate these changes.

10. If you could accomplish one special thing at work, what would that be? What would be the very first step in moving toward that personal goal? Write the two answers down.

WHEN YOU'VE finished your meditation, go to your desk or any place where you can concentrate and work without interruption.

Spread out all the notes you've made and read them over carefully. Take a sheet of paper and divide it into three vertical columns. In the first, write all the positive items from your notes. In the second, list the negatives, and in the third column write down all the action items and add more that may occur to you as you go. The action items should be aimed at bolstering your positives and correcting or at least addressing the negatives.

If you have more items in the positive column than the negative, be grateful for your harmonious work situation. But if you have more negatives listed, don't despair. These just give you more opportunities to put feng shui into practice to improve your career, your relationships at work, and your life.

No matter how long a list you might have of either positives or negatives, work to make sure you still have a good number of action items. Otherwise, you will be stuck in limbo, with nowhere to go and no way to improve your career or strive for greater business success!

Taking the time to do these exercises will help you achieve balance and harmony within yourself. And once this has been accomplished, you will have a much easier time balancing the chi of your surroundings. Faithful practice will build and enhance your chi, gradually bringing you closer to the ideal you have envisioned.

As your personal chi is being strengthened, you may begin to be more graceful in your interactions with others and to feel compassion and generosity in dealing with them. Gradually you may find yourself in positions of power beyond what you might have envisioned in the beginning. It all comes from chi—and it all begins with you.

Tim Ryan loved his job designing software, but he hated going to work every morning. As a deeply shy person, Tim did not enjoy casual interactions with his co-workers and was often at odds with them. Although he meant no particular harm, Tim gave off an air of impatience, discomfort, and awkwardness whenever he was approached. And he was not treated particularly well in return.

Tim became fascinated with feng shui and devoted himself to learning everything he could. Among his discoveries was the concept of personal chi. He learned that his own chi was weak and that he was almost always out of balance with his environment and his colleagues because of it. As a meticulous person, Tim did an excellent job of goal setting and worked diligently on several of the exercises I shared with him. He zeroed in on his strengths and weaknesses and figured out what would improve his attitude toward work. The first thing he did was build up his personal chi and, in conjunction with that, his self-confidence. With his new self-confidence, Tim was able to persuade his boss to allow him to telecommute four days a week. He now works at home Monday through Thursday and only goes to the office on Friday for meetings and to do paperwork. He is able to enjoy the occasional social interaction with co-workers and has even discovered he shares a passion for baseball with many office colleagues. This new common ground recently led to an invitation to join the office softball team.

OFFICE ENVIRONMENTS often have too much yang energy. The hard surfaces, metal equipment and file cabinets, glaring fluorescent lights, and active bustling environment can agitate and exhaust everyone who works there. This, in turn, causes low morale, hasty decision making, incoherent business policies, and angry arguments among employees. Generally speaking, intensely yang workplaces cause people to feel tense most of the time, adding to the stress of the workplace.

If you aren't sure where your workplace falls on the yin/yang continuum, that could mean it is in balance. But just to be certain, ask yourself these questions:

1. Is the light too bright? (This includes sunlight streaming in.)
2. Are there piles of papers, stacks of boxes, and other materials lying around and getting in the way?
3. Is it usually too warm?
4. Is it noisy?
5. Does it sometimes smell bad?
6. Does environmental noise disturb workers?
7. Is the atmosphere hectic to the point of being hard to keep up with?
8. Does the office feel crowded and cramped?
9. Do co-workers argue frequently?
10. Do men dominate the workplace to the exclusion of women decision makers?

Each of these conditions is a symptom of too much yang. It could mean your office or workplace is being flooded with more chi than it can process and circulate. This causes bad chi and tends to create excess in all things. Any one of these symptoms should signal you to add more yin wherever you can because yang can be particularly destructive.

With too much yang, discussions can become heated or aggressive, escalating in some cases to raised voices and angry, insulting

YIN AND YANG BALANCE: CREATING AN ENVIRONMENT THAT INSPIRES TRUST exchanges among colleagues. This is not only unpleasant and unproductive, it is an indication of very bad feng shui; the environment is seriously out of balance.

Overall, the yang atmosphere is not conducive to good decision making or sound business practices and can result in lost opportunities and bad financial outcomes for the business. Too much yang is bad for morale and encourages employee turnover, which can cost a company huge amounts of money in lost revenue and employee hiring and training costs.

On the other hand, some "luxury" offices go too far in the other direction. Heavy carpeting and draperies, hushed tones, subdued lighting, dark furniture—all these symbols of quiet good taste will throw off the balance with too much yin energy. These offices may suffer from lack of leadership, low productivity, stalled decision making, and meanness and backbiting among employees. This out-of-balance yin is frustrating for everyone who works there. Employees in this environment will be on edge and suspicious of coworkers and managers alike.

If you work in an office similar to either of these, find ways to counteract the imbalance with touches of yin or yang as needed. Try to add these balancing touches to common areas if you can, but at the very least, make sure you balance your own office or work space. You will then preside over an environment where others feel safe. They will sense that your office is a sanctuary of serenity amid the chaos. Colleagues and superiors alike will tend to trust you. Your projects, plans, and proposals will be regarded with favor and you will be singled out for praise and promotion.

If you are the supervisor or manager in an office with such problems, make it a priority to get yin and yang in balance. You will see morale improve quickly and your stock as a good manager will go up.

To correct an overly yang environment, add touches of softness, darkness, and quiet. A large green floor plant will bring yin to the room, as will desk lamps that soften the overhead light, throw pillows, or any personal effects that add a sense of peace to the room. Slow down the pace, clean up any clutter crowding the area, add subdued touches and soft colors and objects—these are the basics for bringing yin into a yang atmosphere.

A yin office, on the other hand, will need color, activity, sound, and light. This can require some ingenuity if you're in a conservative corporate environment. But a bright red pen, a distinctive silver or gold picture frame, a solid rock paperweight, or even multicolored diskettes will allow you to add unobtrusive yang elements here and there.

A balanced and harmonious environment can encourage congenial relationships no matter where you are. Eating in expensive and elegant restaurants makes people feel good, but the experience goes far beyond the food. The carefully arranged decor—lighting, wall color, flowers, place settings—all contribute to the welcoming aura that allows people to feel good about themselves and their companions. It's not a coincidence that couples frequently choose "romantic" restaurants such as these to celebrate special occasions or to pursue a courtship. You just don't get the same feelings from loud, brightly lit, bustling restaurants, even though the food is often just as good!

TAKING COMMAND

BY POSITIONING yourself carefully within any room you can exert a certain degree of control over the way your supervisors and colleagues respond to you, and even over the proceedings at a meeting. Just as careful feng shui can bring wealth your way, it can also bring you power and authority.

- To be at your most powerful at a meeting, arrive early and take a seat that faces the door and is as far inside the room as possible. In this spot you have control—you can see everything going on, while keeping your eye on the door. You will suffer no uncomfortable surprises in this position, and no one else in the room will rival you for command of the meeting.

· To put people at ease in your office or at a meeting in a conference room, allow them at least a partial view of the door or out a window. But never do this at the expense of your own commanding position.

· To ensure that people who come to your office are confident in your abilities, make sure yin and yang are in balance and that the aesthetics and "grooming" of your office are impeccable. You lose power if your domain gives the impression that you are not in control of every aspect of your job.

· To maintain a balanced atmosphere, keep an even number of chairs in your office or conference room. Even if you think you need only three chairs, add a fourth. This will provide balance and harmony while suggesting that your office is a center of activity. But don't do this if it will overcrowd the room. It's more important to allow space for the chi to flow.

FURNITURE ARRANGEMENT AND WORKPLACE RELATIONSHIPS

CO-WORKERS WHOSE desks face each other directly are apt to bicker and compete. If you can't move the two facing desks, create a barrier between the desks; a living plant will block your direct view while giving the benefit of positive chi. In the San Francisco interior design offices of Joan Osburn, two drafting tables sat opposite each other for years, and everyone in the office was negatively affected by the constant tension between the two draftspeople. In a major office renovation, the drafting tables were replaced with new tables, which both faced the door. The entire atmosphere changed as the two colleagues began to share ideas and cooperate with each other.

When two employees share an office and one employee's desk is closer to the door, that person will end up in a subordinate role. Remember, the farther inside the office you sit, the more power you have. The dynamic of relative power is at work here: Not only will the person closest to the door be seen as less powerful, he will also have less understanding of the business than his colleague.

It is absolutely critical to pay attention to this principle when a boss and an employee share an office. The employee may become insubordinate and may usurp the power of a supervisor who sits in the vulnerable position closest to the door.

PERSONAL RELATIONSHIPS AND ROMANCE

THE SOUTHWEST, as you'll recall, governs not only love, romance, and marriage, it also holds sway over mother-child relationships and partnerships. If you want to get along better with your colleagues or even your spouse, by all means take advantage of the southwest area of your office. (Since you spend so much of your time here, enhancing your office can bring powerful results in all aspects of your professional or personal life.) If you are looking forward to starting a business on your own someday and need a business partner, this is the area to focus on. And if, despite all the bad press office romances get, you'd still like to attract a significant other from down the hall, use some discreet enhancements in your office.

Make each enhancement specific to your goal. And be as creative as possible in bringing colors, elements, numbers, celestial animals, and inspiring images into your arrangements. Here are a few examples.

- If you want to attract a romantic partner, keep fresh yellow flowers in the southwest area.
- To strengthen or repair an existing relationship with a colleague, family member, or important friend, hang a pair of earthenware planters with healthy green plants on the southwest wall. The planters bring the earth element to the southwest and the green plants add chi. Using the pots in pairs adds strength to the enhancement because 2 is the number associated with the southwest.

· If you hope to acquire a serious business partner for an upcoming venture, find images that represent your business goal and place them in pairs in a southwest corner. Try including the phoenix in this area, as this is the celestial animal that represents new beginnings.

As always when working with any feng shui enhancements, don't forget to do the footwork—take practical action to clear the path toward your goal. If you're looking for friendships or romance, check that you've got the basics down: make sure you're a good listener and by all means, check your teeth for spinach after lunch! A field of yellow tulips cannot overcome the obstacles of a grouchy, unpleasant, or ill-groomed person searching for companionship!

MORE THAN ACCESSORIES

THE OBJECTS you surround yourself with at work can do more than simply decorate your office or remind you of a favorite vacation. Every item you choose has the potential to help you realize your goals. Your office accessories can draw healthy and positive chi into your workplace or direct negative, harmful chi away from you. When you use the five fundamental elements, the eight life areas of the bagua, and carefully chosen symbols, your decor will give your career goals a major boost while it lends an air of distinction to your work space.

Your office needn't look like a Chinese curio shop or a New Age emporium to create good feng shui. There is a wide range of decorating possibilities that can bring harmony and balance without attracting any attention other than aesthetic admiration. This chapter will guide you in selecting lighting, color, artwork, flowers and plants, and an array of common and uncommon office accessories to enhance your work environment and help you reach your professional goals.

LIGHTING

GOOD LIGHT is crucial to good feng shui. Good feng shui, as well as entirely practical considerations, dictates that you have adequate light when you work. The better (not necessarily the brighter) the lighting, the stronger and more vibrant the chi that surrounds you.

Whether it comes from an unshaded window or bad overhead lighting, avoid glare at all costs. Glare is not only a major irritant and distraction, it's also a source of sha chi. If you're not able to block glare coming at you—from afternoon sun pouring through a large window, for example—hang a crystal in the path of the glare. The crystal will catch and refract the light, creating rainbows and breaking up the sha chi.

Harsh and unforgiving overhead lighting will quickly dissipate healthy chi and replace it with sha. Even if the overhead lighting is bright, place an attractive lamp on your desk. The lamp should be in proportion to the size of your desk, neither taking up room you need to work, nor looming too high above the desktop. This softer light will dissipate the overly strong chi, but still allow for healthy chi circulation. And at the same time it can make your work space seem more personal and inviting. You will automatically feel more at home at your desk and anyone who drops by—from bosses to colleagues—will register this fact approvingly.

Place the lamp so its light comes from the side opposite your dominant hand. If you're right-handed, for example, and the lamp is on the right, your hand will block the illumination coming from that side. But your writing hand won't be in the path of the light if the lamp is on your left, and you'll benefit from the power of the uninterrupted light.

Floor lamps often cast an attractive light without taking up any space on your desk. A torchère that softly illuminates the wall and ceiling above it will draw the chi high up in your office and stimulate your creativity by raising the positive energy.

Crystal or glass chandeliers are almost always a perfect feng shui enhancement because they combine beautiful lighting with the chi-enhancing properties of many light-catching facets.

YOU MAY or may not feel comfortable displaying natural crystals in your office, but you can get the same chi-energizing effect with the much more traditional office accouterment, the crystal paperweight. Chandeliers, mobiles, or any glittering glass object can also stand in for hanging crystals. Any of these can catch and disperse the light in your office, boosting good chi. Because they are such a strong earth element, crystals can be used in the southwest to help you reach your goal of solidifying business partnerships, attracting a spouse, or strengthening the bonds of any important relationship.

CRYSTALS AND CHIMES

If you wish more clients would call, hang a crystal over your telephone to activate the chi energy. If, on the other hand, you're having trouble keeping up with calls, put a rock or other heavy object next to the phone to keep it from ringing as often. The density and weight of the object will stabilize the energy surrounding the telephone.

Wind chimes are popular in feng shui for attracting chi with their movement and pleasant tinkling sounds. But it is bad luck to hang them indoors. So if you like them and want to incorporate them into your feng shui plan, be sure to hang them outside where they'll catch a breeze and send their tinkling sounds into the wind.

COLOR CREATES the mood and sets a tone for any environment. If you're able to select paint for your office, your first goal should be to use color to establish a feeling of harmony and peace. Start with a soft

COLOR

background shade, then use more vibrant colors as accents, always keeping your eye on the life aspiration areas you want to highlight, as well as the purpose of the area you are decorating.

Pediatrician Karen Elson in Falls Church, Virginia, painted the waiting room of her office a soft pastel green, because of the color's association with health and growth. She then accented a special play corner with bright white (the color for children) and blue (another shade representing health and growth). The effect is lively enough to be attractive to children, yet calming enough to soothe anxious parents.

Harold Berg, an architect in Brooklyn, New York, painted his entire suite of offices pale yellow. He explained that good relationships with his clients are central to his business so he chose the color that corresponds to the relationship area. Harold then used accents of orange fabric and pale wood furniture, particularly in the southwest sector, where the earth tones are especially beneficial.

Keep in mind that you can use colors to invoke the five fundamental elements, which is one more way to encourage these powerful forces to help achieve your goals. For example:

- Deep blue can be a good alternative to black in symbolizing water, if you want to accent the element of the north for your career aspirations.
- To highlight fire in the south, use red, of course, but also pinks and deep maroons.
- To activate the east, use light browns, which symbolize wood for growth, or use clear greens and light blues that will bring spring to mind.
- The metal element, which will work wonders for your creativity aspirations in the west, can be invoked with white, but also with the gold and silver of picture frames, and desk accessories such as clocks and bookends.

· Use browns, oranges, deep yellows, and tans to invoke earth in the southwest.

ORGANIZE WITH COLOR

I HAVE often used the lowly paper clip as an effective feng shui enhancement in my own office. Multicolored plastic-coated clips can be used to color-coordinate your clipping according to the goal you have for the document. I use red clips on anything I send out having to do with publicity (fame) or my reputation. Yellow or orange clips are reserved for items associated with relationships or persons of great importance (remember that yellow is the color of royalty), purple clips are on all my financially related paperwork, and green or blue clips accompany papers that are intended to help my professional growth, inspire creativity, or open new doors. Paper clip feng shui works equally well whether you are sending items to someone else or merely arranging them in your own files. Colored file folders can work the same way. Focus on your goal for a particular set of papers and consciously select the colored clip or folder that corresponds to your wishes.

ARTWORK AND ACCESSORIES

THE MOST important thing to keep in mind when choosing art for your office is that it should somehow depict your aspirations and lift your spirits. Surround yourself with joyful images and at all costs avoid art that is dark, dreary, confusing, or distressing. It isn't necessary to invest much money to buy something truly lovely and special. You can frequently find beautiful and inspiring artwork at the gift store of your favorite museum. Or purchase a commemorative poster from an event that you especially enjoyed.

Children's book writer Marcy Hinsdale keeps a poster from a New York City book fair hanging over her desk. It shows children accompanied by dinosaurs riding on the pages of open books, flying over the city's skyline at twilight. Marcy glances at it many times a day and finds joy and inspiration for her writing every time she looks up.

And don't overlook calendar art as a potential source of feng shui enhancements. A good bookstore with a wide selection of calendars will provide you with an enormous array of scenes, symbols, and subjects—virtually anything pertaining to your goals and dreams.

Imaginative computer and desk accessories can have the impact of art in your office. Mouse pads now come decorated with everything from cartoon characters to Dutch Old Master reproductions. Have fun with these, keeping in mind the colors they incorporate and any elements their images may symbolize. Screen savers are another fun and potentially auspicious office accessory. You can even get a screen saver "aquarium," with colorful fish floating serenely by, enhancing your prospects for financial and career success. As an added bonus, this is one fish tank you won't have to keep clean! Those flying toasters are cute, but keep in mind that they add more metal to your computer, which could create an imbalance of elements, depending on where your computer sits and what else is around it.

If you have a feng shui enhancement in mind that calls for a special element, bookends can provide exactly what you're looking for. You can find bookends in wood, metal, or earth (stone), or you can use large wax candles as bookends to represent fire, or clear heavy glass to add the element of water. Many well-stocked bookstores carry a selection of bookends and, once again, your museum gift shop or catalog may come in handy for locating this item.

CHINESE GOOD FORTUNE SYMBOLS

THE CHINESE make great use of symbolism and enjoy calling on the mystical properties of animals, birds, flowers, and other special objects for luck and prosperity. Use these symbols in your office in any form that works for you, from artwork to doorstops.

Of course, you needn't feel that only Asian art will bring you good feng shui. In fact, it is important that you draw on your own background and taste to find artwork that is meaningful to you. But if you do have a taste for Chinese or other Asian art, this section will guide you in interpreting its symbols and selecting just the right piece for your purposes.

FISH, AS we've seen, represent money and abundance. In Chinese art-work they are occasionally used to represent success. Look for fish on Chinese vases and in paintings of fishermen with freshly caught fish.

FISH

    If you can't put an aquarium in your office or a pond just outside your door, display fish in any artful form (paintings, statues, tapestries, screen savers) that suits your office environment and pleases your eye. Carp and goldfish are popular choices. But stay away from angel fish because their angled shape shoots poison arrows in all directions. And as you can most likely guess, piranhas or other predatory fish bring very bad feng shui!

BIRDS ARE excellent representations of good fortune, fame, creativity, and various other blessings.

BIRDS

- The mythical phoenix (directly associated with south and fame and fortune) evokes creativity. The phoenix is destroyed by flames only to re-create himself and rise again from the ashes— a good reminder that you should never let obstacles keep you from trying again.
- The glamorous and dignified peacock can convey these prop-erties to you when you exhibit images of the bird or even bright blue and green peacock feathers at appropriate spots in your work space.
- Another excellent bird for attracting fortune and fame is the brilliant red cardinal. Display him in paintings, vases, photos, or any other aesthetic representations that appeal to you.

- Believe it or not, bats are money symbols and represent good luck in Chinese art. They are often painted red and hung upside down in Chinese homes to attract good fortune. Occasionally they are used as symbols of wisdom because by hanging upside down they are able to see things from another perspective.
- Even the common canary can symbolize and attract wealth with its bright gold color. You needn't keep a live one caged at work (which could be messy and difficult). Look for the peppy little domestic bird depicted in paintings, figurines, or small artworks.

ANIMALS

- The most important animal in Chinese tradition is the mystical and powerful dragon. He can bring you inspiration, wealth, and protection, any of which can be essential for advancing your career and promoting general business success.
- The horse is one of the Seven Treasures of Buddhism and symbolizes speed and perseverance, two other qualities vital to long-term success in the business world.
- The tiger is the strongest of the celestial animals, but also the most violent. The tiger represents the violence in human nature and can both defend and attack. He will always spring into action when provoked. Because he is wild and fierce, keep him where you can see him at all times, lest he devour you when you're not looking.
- If it's stability you require, the tortoise is an excellent choice. With its own sturdy shell and famously slow but steady pace, the tortoise is known for staying power and longevity. He will assist in long-term projects and keep you safe from attacks from the rear. This unassuming little reptile can be a true friend to your career, especially when you place him in the north, the direction of career and business success.

- The snake is very clever and is known for timely and wise action. He can be your ally in wisdom and tactical decision making. It's up to you to find a clever way to keep a symbolic snake at your side without frightening squeamish co-workers!
- Frogs are symbolic of good fortune, and frog figurines are often placed near the front door in Chinese homes to signify the arrival of wealth. If you're lucky, you might even be able to find a little frog statue with a coin in its mouth—an especially effective symbol of money coming into your life. Put one near the inside door of your office or near the entrance to your business (look for frog-shaped doorstops) and marvel as money hops through your front door.

THERE IS no such thing as an unlucky plant or flower (although cactuses are the least auspicious because of their prickly nature). Many flowers have special significance in Chinese lore, however, and you might want to draw upon these in your decorating-for-success scheme.

FLOWERS AND PLANTS

- The peony, which is depicted in many beautiful Chinese paintings and screens, is a symbol of good fortune and long life. It is frequently used to represent wealth and honor.
- The chrysanthemum represents happiness and laughter. Along with the peony, it is seen everywhere during the Chinese New Year celebrations.
- Irises come in the exact shade of purple to activate your wealth corner in an extremely powerful way.
- The lotus is the sacred flower of Buddhism. It is impractical to have a live one around your office because it grows on muddy ponds. But you can draw on its blessings of peace, purity, and spiritual growth by surrounding yourself with its image on pottery or in other artwork.

- The plum blossom plant attracts uncommonly positive and vigorous chi flow. Plant it outside your business or the building you work in and bask in the results.
- Sunflowers, in their shade of striking golden yellow, can bring yang to a dark, dull, all-yin room.
- Green plants are excellent for activating any areas of the room that correspond to your aspirations. And they are very effective when used to block sha chi that radiates from square posts or sharp-edged furniture in an interior space.
- Red geraniums are thought to attract prosperity and are a popular feng shui flower. They are easy to grow indoors as long as you keep the pot in the sun. They'll love the natural light of a south-facing window and their color will complement your area of fame and fortune.

Flowers and plants must be healthy and thriving to bring you their positive influences. When flowers die or plants wither, throw them out or replace them immediately. You may use silk flowers and plants, but keep them dusted and bright-looking.

Dried flowers are thought by some to have very bad feng shui because they have lost their essence from lack of water. However, I've seen many thriving enterprises decorated attractively with dried wreath and flower arrangements, especially when the colors stay bright. See what works for you, but if you have trouble you can't trace, by all means discard any dried blooms.

FAMOUS OFFICES—
Feng Shui at Work on the Careers
of Some Well-known People

WHETHER THEY'VE heard of it or not, feng shui has affected the lives and influenced the careers of plumbers and presidents, tycoons and television personalities. Not only has good or bad feng shui had a role in directing individual professional lives, its influence has spread, like ripples on a pond, to the lives of those surrounding them.

Just for fun—and to keep your newly acquired feng shui sensibilities sharp—take a look at these famous offices and the effect their feng shui has had on their occupants.

WE ALL know Murphy Brown, the sitcom character played by Candice Bergen, whose fictional career as a television journalist has dominated television comedy for the past several years. Murphy Brown may be a fictional character, but her forceful personality has taken on a life of its own: Just remember how real life and fiction blended when Vice President Dan Quayle denounced Murphy's lifestyle as a negative moral example for the nation! Real-life journalists take Murphy seriously also, appearing frequently on the program.

MURPHY BROWN—
PERFECT POWER
POSITION

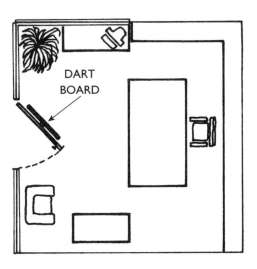

DART
BOARD

Although the show's producers probably never thought of it when they designed Murphy's office, the feng shui of her work space seems tailor-made for the character's professional strengths and weaknesses. The set designers intuitively reflected her powerful—yet flawed—personality in the arrangement of her office. Her desk faces the door and her back is to a solid wall, putting her in a strong power position. She has a bowl of fish on the forward edge of her desk, encouraging abundance and financial success. The walls behind and around her desk are packed with awards and memorabilia symbolizing her accomplishments. These mementos of former professional success add a positive element to her surroundings, keeping the chi level up and pushing her toward ever more professional triumphs.

But if the positive aspects of Murphy Brown's life and career seem to spring from feng shui, so do the negative. Because her desk is in a straight line with the office door, she is regularly bombarded with sha chi. This powerful negative force may account for her famous bad temper as well as the character and plot complications that bedevil her weekly!

THE OVAL Office is another workplace familiar to Americans, even though most of us have never set foot in it. Did you ever wonder why its occupant often has such a tough time getting congressional support for his proposals? You can't put the blame entirely on partisan politics. The leader of the free world is coping with some pretty bad feng shui at work.

Notice the window you see right behind the president's desk whenever he speaks to the nation from the Oval Office. Without a solid wall behind him, he is robbed of solid support for his policies. At the same time, the window allows valuable chi energy to escape behind him. And it's not just a badly placed window that depletes the president's chi. The room also has too many entrances and exits. Four doors open into the room and cause an erratic pattern of chi flow, disrupting the concentration of the president and his advisers whenever they confer in that room. Even more important, the president's power is dissipated by this disrupted chi flow, so he's constantly being second-guessed. He could quickly improve his lot by doing several things: move the desk away from the window; seal off one of the four doors; and put plants near the fireplace to balance the fire element and "take the heat off."

THE OVAL OFFICE— WEAK CHI FOR THE CHIEF

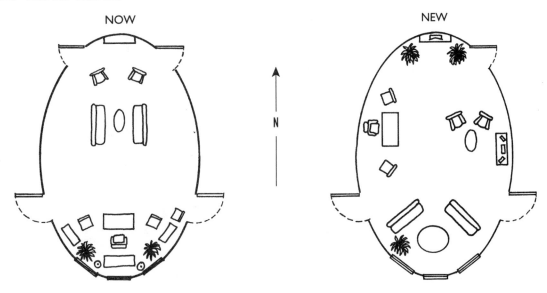

NOW

NEW

N

THOMAS
JEFFERSON—
FENG SHUI AND
DIFFICULTIES
AT MONTICELLO

THOMAS JEFFERSON, the third president of the United States, was also a farmer, inventor, statesman, political philosopher, revolutionary, and—not least among his multiple talents—architect. Monticello, the Charlottesville, Virginia, home Jefferson designed, lived in, and worked and died in, is considered part of his autobiographical legacy.

The cabinet (as Jefferson called his study) is an unusual room, shaped like half an octagon, and projecting as a bay from his sleeping quarters. Tall windows and a set of French doors let in plenty of light. Jefferson made the most of the available sunlight by designing a revolving writing table and chair that permitted him to turn as he worked, catching the sun as it moved across the sky. Also in the interest of efficiency, Jefferson put his alcove bed adjacent to the cabinet room so he could get to work as soon as he rose in the morning.

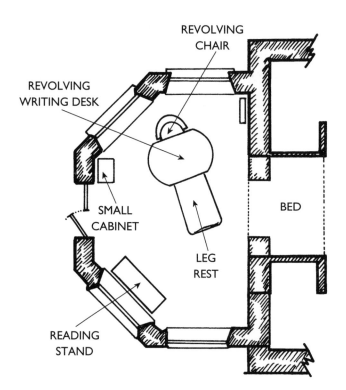

Experimentation and invention were at the heart of Jefferson's designs, and his cabinet/sleeping room reflected these passions. Unfortunately, Jefferson's enthusiasms sometimes clashed with principles of good feng shui. The incompatible chi energy of his sleeping and working areas interfered with his sleep at night and made it difficult for him to concentrate on fiscal matters during the day. Even more seriously, the odd half-octagon shape of his office may have further contributed to his financial problems. A full eight-sided construction would have been ideal, since eight represents prosperity and the octagonal shape, which symbolizes the ba-gua, is highly auspicious. In effect, Jefferson's experimental design slashed in half his opportunity for prosperity. Of course, this unfortunate feng shui was exacerbated by Jefferson's rather profligate spending habits and a legendary generosity that continued even when he had little money to be generous with.

Chi, the life-giving force, was severely depleted throughout Jefferson's house, and especially in his study, as Jefferson became more and more distracted by his depressed economic situation; the house and its furnishings fell into shockingly shabby condition. At the time of Jefferson's death, this great man and brilliant thinker was so deeply in debt that the entire estate was sold off to pay his creditors.

IT'S HARD to argue with success. Donald Trump, president and CEO of Trump Organization, and one of the richest men in the world, is the personification of peak performance in business. But he's had a secret advantage for several years, since he began consulting feng shui masters for all his important projects. Because Trump does a great deal of business in Asia, he's made it his business to surround himself with good feng shui. As Trump has famously said, if feng shui is important to his clients, "that's good enough for me."

DONALD TRUMP— GOOD FENG SHUI PAYS DIVIDENDS

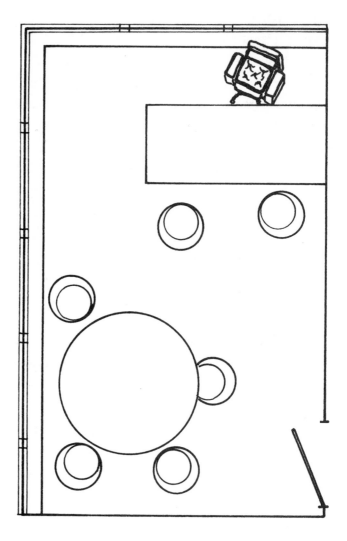

Trump's enormous Manhattan office is a classic example of practical feng shui in a work environment. Trump values the spectacular view from his office window but wisely faces the office door, rather than the window, while seated at his desk. He compensates for the window behind his desk—which might leave him without support from behind—by sitting in a high-backed leather desk chair. And he's further supported by symbolic dragons and tigers in the form of skyscrapers immediately behind him. Just like the protecting hills of ancient feng shui practice, the tall buildings shield Trump from danger.

A beige carpet provides a restful background, while red velvet circular chairs invoke the colors of luxury and wealth (Trump's desk chair was also carefully chosen to represent luxury; it's covered with a rich burgundy leather). The auspiciously shaped circular chairs are dotted throughout the room and encourage gentle yet vibrant chi flow. The large round conference table continues the gently curving pattern, while it also promotes harmony among the people who conduct meetings there. Donald Trump obviously values the benefits good office feng shui has bestowed on him, and has said, with uncharacteristic understatement, "This particular building has been lucky for me."

FINAL THOUGHTS

IT'S NO coincidence that the popularity of feng shui has surged tremendously in the past few years. This ancient art is answering a modern need to gain some control over lives that often move faster than any of us would like.

It's encouraging to see that our society, while focusing as much as ever on progress and technological achievement, is coming to value an art that can't always be explained logically. As the pace of life intensifies—e-mail, faxes, cell phones, video conferencing, longer work hours—there's a measure of comfort in the knowledge that a somewhat mystical phenomenon can help us establish a connection with the natural world and its rhythms.

A word of caution: Feng shui isn't magic. Invoking its ancient wisdom is no substitute for dealing with practical realities like balancing your checkbook. And even the most skilled feng shui master will not be able to solve all your problems by moving your furniture. But practicing feng shui definitely provides an opportunity to reach beyond the mundane and to stretch the limits of possibility. The first challenge is to imagine what might be possible and go from there. Don't think of the practice of feng shui as moving furniture. Think of it as rearranging your life, from the inside out.

KIRSTEN M. LAGATREE is the author of the best-selling *Feng Shui: Arranging Your Home to Change Your Life* and the coauthor of *The Home Office Secret: How to Balance Your Professional and Personal Lives While Working at Home*. She is a writer based in the Washington, D.C., area.